PT
395
.L3
1967

Lange, Victor.
Modern German literature,
1870-1940.

MODERN GERMAN LITERATURE

MODERN GERMAN LITERATURE

1870 - 1940

VICTOR LANGE

KENNIKAT PRESS, INC./PORT WASHINGTON, N. Y.

MODERN GERMAN LITERATURE

Reissued in 1967 by Kennikat Press by arrangement

Library of Congress Catalog Card No: 67-27616

Manufactured in the United States of America

TO *HERBERT DAVIS*

Aber Freund! wir kommen zu spät; zwar leben die Götter,
Aber über dem Haupt droben in anderer Welt.
Endlos wirken sie da und scheinen's wenig zu achten,
Ob wir leben, so sehr schonen die Himmlischen uns.
Denn nicht immer vermag ein schwaches Gefäss sie zu fassen,
Nur zuzeiten erträgt göttliche Fülle der Mensch.
Traum von ihnen ist drauf das Leben, aber das Irrsal
Hilft, wie Schlummer, und stark machet die Not und die Nacht,
Bis dass Helden genug in der ehernen Wiege gewachsen,
Herzen an Kraft, wie sonst, ähnlich den Himmlischen sind.
Donnernd kommen sie drauf. Indessen dünket mir öfters
Besser zu schlafen, wie so ohne Genossen zu sein,
So zu harren, und was zu tun indes und zu sagen
Weiss ich nicht, und wozu Dichter in dürftiger Zeit?
Aber sie sind, sagst du, wie des Weingotts heilige Priester,
Welche von Lande zu Land zogen in heiliger Nacht.

HÖLDERLIN

PREFACE

THE following essay is intended to supply a critical outline of German literature between 1870 and the present. It should appeal especially to those who are not familiar with the details of that literature's recent history and who do not read the originals with ease. So general an aim may seem not only ambitious but possibly unpromising, and it involves, without doubt, certain difficulties which it is well to recognize clearly. Any attempt to establish historical and critical cohesion beyond the mere fortuitous mosaic of events is a matter of interpretation; and interpretation will not succeed if we aim, even obliquely, at deceptive completeness or dry detachment. For completeness is a professorial virtue which it is wisest not to strain, and detachment is nowhere less valid an attitude than in the contemplation and interpretation of literature. On the contrary, literary criticism, even though its immediate object is the specifically verbal work of art with its inescapable and telling medium, is seldom true and alive unless it ventures judgments which go beyond the primary aesthetic experience. Literary criticism must not fail to be a mode of action; it requires, as well as technical knowledge, the readiness of a decision.

Broad strokes, and even generalizations, have therefore seemed preferable to that distracting abundance of names, titles, and dates which is sometimes supposed to constitute the awkward weave of literary history; and an occasional oversimplification has been inevitable. Those who are acquainted with the particulars of the German literary scene may not be reconciled to some omissions; others may, rightly, protest that certain authors have been treated either too meanly or too enthusiastically. But the scope and intention of this essay would be seriously misjudged if undue demands were to be made upon it.

An exhaustive list of the translated works of the authors discussed will be found in the Bibliography, together with references to some of the more generally illuminating critical studies available in English.

In the text itself all titles are cited in the original, but English translations are given in a separate index of titles.

Mr. Alfred A. Knopf has kindly allowed me to quote the passage preceding Chapter III, from Thomas Mann's "Goethe and Tolstoy," *Three Essays,* 1929, pp. 136–137. The other chapter mottoes come from the following sources: p. vii, Hölderlin, "Brot und Wein," VII, *Werke,* ed. W. Böhm, 1909, II, 318; p. 1, Goethe,

Maximen und Reflexionen, ed. M. Hecker ("Schriften der Goethe-Gesellschaft," XXI), 1907, no. 666; p. 31, Nietzsche, "Richard Wagner in Bayreuth," *The Complete Works,* ed. O. Levy, I, 1 (1910), 123; p. 77, Donne, "First Anniversary," *The Poems,* ed. H. J. C. Grierson, 1912, I, 237–238; p. 93, Novalis, *Fragmente,* ed. E. Kamnitzer, 1929, no. 1181; p. 113, E. R. Curtius, *Deutscher Geist in Gefahr,* 1932, p. 27.

Parts of the material here presented were originally written for the forthcoming *Dictionary of Modern European Literature,* and for permission to reprint some of those passages I owe thanks to the Columbia University Press. My colleagues, R. C. Bald and H. Schneider, have been kind enough to read the proofs and have offered many valuable suggestions. I am especially grateful to Miss Virginia Seery, who has, with unfailing generosity, helped in the preparation of this book.

V. L.

Ithaca, New York
Spring, 1945

CONTENTS

MODERN GERMAN LITERATURE

THE eighteenth century is commonly praised for its analytical preoccupation. To the nineteenth the task now remains of discovering the false syntheses which prevail and of analyzing their contents anew.

GOETHE

I

PERSPECTIVES

THE historical events of the nineteenth century, so far-reaching in scope and so radical in their social and intellectual consequences, gave to the writings of the age a unity of perception which it would be difficult to discover in any of the earlier periods of European literary history. The Napoleonic wars, the implications of the industrial revolution, and the ominous emergence of new continental powers became matters of the deepest common concern to those European men of letters who recognized in the incidents of history the signs of an alarming transformation of manners and ideas. It was a century of unparalleled action, but at the same time of a vigorous creative intelligence in which philosophers and artists alike had their share. Startling economic and political changes compelled the men of letters to venture into new areas of interest and to develop unprecedented forms of expression. It is true that the poet was no longer sustained, as he had been in the ages of faith and reason, by the humanistic assumption of the unity of man. But the uniformity of the European world was evident enough, and in the simultaneous intellectual movements of the time the common anxiety can be felt with which all European poets regarded the challenges of the century. The romantic or the naturalistic sensibilities and the phases of enthusiasm or disillusionment for which the English, French, and German writers developed their specific national idiom sprang clearly from impulses which were not confined to the limits of the national life.

If it seems paradoxical to stress the unity of the European experience at a time when nationalistic aspirations asserted themselves with aggressive self-confidence, it will be no less surprising to realize that one of the cardinal themes of this century, in which the powers of the middle class were being steadily consolidated, was the attack persistently leveled by the poets and critics upon the very tenets of bourgeois life. The evidence of the crisis in values, which is only now about to reach its climax, was everywhere apparent, even though in England and France the structure of the social order, fundamentally strong and flexible, was perhaps less dangerously shaken by the threats of revolutionary criticism than it was elsewhere. In Germany the balance of political life was more precariously maintained, and it was only natural that there the middle class, which had established itself with such militant efficiency, should have offered a ready target for ever more savage attacks upon its own beliefs. But as the German writer by his revolutionary insight sought to emancipate himself from the bourgeois tenets of the century, he assumed at the same time a public responsibility within the political life of the nation such as he had never before been able to maintain.

The climate of the early nineteenth century in Germany had, on the whole, not been favorable for the work of the artist. To foreign observers like the sympathetic and intelligent English and American visitors, the world of the twenties and thirties appeared almost idyllic—a provincial world of barely twenty million inhabitants, of small attractive rural towns, of an imaginative middle class, of a serenely happy landscape and enchanting romantic melodies: the world of Weimar and Heidelberg, of the brothers Grimm, and Uhland, of Eichendorff's *Taugenichts* and Weber's *Freischütz.*

But harsh winds had begun to blow from the west, carrying with them religious and political doctrines which a nation that had scarcely adjusted itself to the overpowering experience of the European wars found impossible to judge with a steady mind. For, at the same time, all thinking and feeling was being peremptorily forced into the rigid authoritarianism of the Metternich regime.

To be sure, the more decisive changes in the intellectual situation did not go unrecognized; to so resolute and circumspect a historian of German literature as

G. G. Gervinus, it seemed, even in 1835, that the age of the poet had come to an end. Three years after Goethe's death he insisted that the function of the literary artist was bound to assume new forms in order to adjust itself to the changing life of the nation. In Heine, in Grabbe, and in Büchner a new type of writer, profoundly different from Carlyle's Goethe-inspired image of the hero as poet, was about to emerge, his eyes no longer fastened upon the identity of man, but rather upon the problematical aspects of the particular social situation.

Once before, when the serious political consequences of the defeat of Jena in 1806 had compelled the younger romantics to reassess their intellectual position, the direction of their poetical imagination had simultaneously undergone a significant change. Now, a generation later, a series of passionately conceived but disastrously unsuccessful rebellions released across the whole of Europe the long-denied currents of democratic aspirations; again the writers of the late forties found themselves dislocated and without a truly sustaining sense of inner or outer stability.

The effect of the political events upon the German literary scene of the early mid-century was almost completely paralyzing. The lives of the poets who were born shortly after 1800 never came to full fruition. Their work, shaken by the upheavals of the wars of liberation, and at the same time overshadowed by the compelling achievements of Lessing and Humboldt,

Schiller and Goethe, Kant and Schelling, lacks the vigor and independence of critical thinking without which significant literature is difficult to produce. The lingering memories of the idealistic and romantic creed had unnerved, rather than enhanced, their creative will.

In spite of many a remarkable individual work, the total impression of the 1850's is one of frustration and indecision. Even so distinguished a group of dramatists as Grillparzer, Otto Ludwig, and Hebbel succeeded only with difficulty in maintaining themselves against the corroding mood of the age. It is true that five or six of the most revealing collections of post-romantic poetry had appeared in the decade from 1828 to 1838, but in the subsequent thirty years the lyrical achievement, taken as a whole, is scattered and conventional. Among the prose writers the situation is not really different. Indeed, between 1848 and 1870, only two men—Stifter and Keller—contributed to the permanent greatness of the German narrative tradition. Apart from the considerable body of lively memoirs, the most vigorous writing of the period and the most creative intellectual criticism came, not from the novelists, but from the historians and political pamphleteers. There, in Ranke's *Neun Bücher preussischer Geschichte* (1847), in Mommsen's *Römische Geschichte* (1853), in Burckhardt's *Kultur der Renaissance* (1860), or in the early writings of Rudolf Haym (1821–1901, the founder, in 1858, of the

Preussische Jahrbücher), Heinrich von Treitschke (1834–1896), Ferdinand Lassalle (1825–1864), and Paul de Lagarde (1827–1891, *Deutsche Schriften*, 1875–1881), emerges the genuine literary spirit of the mid-century.

If the twenty-five years before 1870 produced in Germany no Dickens or Thackeray, Tennyson or Browning, it was because the German world had not in itself the unity of experience which elsewhere characterized the Victorian generation. With a few interesting but hardly striking exceptions, the novelists, dramatists, and poets chose to keep aloof from the disquieting preoccupation with the new political issues. It was, rather, such revolutionary figures as Wagner, Bismarck, and Karl Marx who established themselves sooner or later in opposition to the crippling forces of a heritage which had become irrelevant. Born in short succession of one another—1813, 1815, and 1818—each of them had, by 1848, at least set out on a spectacular and decisive career.

That the German novelist should have been so ineffective at a critical moment, that he should, even in the future, have continued to be only a minor force, and that his work should never have reached more than a limited European audience is due not merely to the peculiarly narrow range of his subject matter. It should be granted that, because of the political incoherence and, on the other hand, because of the extraordinary variety and richness of the German scene,

German fiction has, throughout its history, been provincial in setting and parochial in its beliefs. Land and people, nature and culture, work and faith, tradition and individualism are there indissolubly interrelated, and in life and art, form an impressive and effective background. In this happy limitation lies the strength and singularity of the German novel, but from it springs at the same time a temptation for the modern novelist to content himself with partial and, as it were, sectional insights into certain pressing contemporary problems. He may, for instance, fail to cope in a significant manner with the emerging social issues. For the urgent and disturbing social themes of the advancing nineteenth century are essentially related to the world of the city, and although the novelist may well view this development from the vantage point of the provincial life, he should not ignore or try to escape from the consequences of the overwhelming economic changes of his age.

It may be that in Germany the capitalistic organization had not, in the sixties and seventies, progressed as decisively as it had in other European countries, but it is not possible to deny its existence. The city, to which the modern novel is inherently bound, had, undoubtedly, by 1860 developed its peculiar and solid pattern of bourgeois living. It was accepted by the philosophical and imaginative writers as the center of far-reaching capitalistic activities. But the radical consequences of this fact do not seem to have become clear to the German novelist, who failed to represent the fundamental issues involved in the urbanization of society. The reason for his failure is not always clearly recognized, but the extent and manner of it are especially remarkable since, even before this period, characteristically aggressive and stirring forms of social fiction had been developed in England and France. There, Balzac and Dickens are in no small degree effective as artists because of their profound insight into the implications of the existing capitalistic forms of behavior. They are at once recorders and critics of an inexorable situation in which all human values are being jeopardized. The German novelist, almost without exception, does not recognize the condition of his own threatened world; he appears to accept the city with pathetic enthusiasm as the very source of national strength, instead of analyzing it as the scene of nearly inevitable social disaster. Friedrich Spielhagen or Gustav Freytag (for many years the cautious editor of the "national-liberal" journal, *Die Grenzboten*) and many other popular novelists, far from being clear-sighted and liberal, rather perpetuate that spirit of bourgeois reaction by which the revolution of 1848 had been so effectively defeated. Even the irresolute sentimentality and false pride in the romantic elements of the German past indicate, among the pseudohistorical authors (Scheffel, Dahn, and Ebers), the condescension and professional detachment of the bourgeois conformists. Wherever the German writer of the generation before Gerhart Hauptmann dealt with pressing social or political issues, he seems to have done so with the self-consciousness of an artist bent primarily upon preserving his character as a "nonpolitical" man.

What social awareness and critical dissent there was can be found, paradoxically enough, in the provinces. There, for more than three generations, the major novelists from Gotthelf to Hermann Stehr provided the most active form of "anticapitalistic" thinking.

Among the novelists writing between 1860 and 1890, Gottfried Keller, Wilhelm Raabe, and Theodor Fontane are the most characteristic representatives of the provincial temper in its most positive form. Each successfully recognizes a stable frame within which the new is being severely and critically viewed: Keller's faith rests in the political life of his Swiss democracy, Raabe delights in the steadfast ways of his old-fashioned folk, and Fontane remains in the confines of either a soundly bourgeois or a precariously aristocratic society.

Fontane's (1819–1898) work is of unusual distinction: by seizing upon the narrow, yet decisive, Prussian scene and by the keenness of his observation, he succeeded in bridging the common gulf between the provincial theme and the craftsmanship of a cosmopolitan storyteller. The motivating elements of his work are a lively sense of historical continuity and a quick perception of the speech and gestures by which the people of his world reveal their particular virtues. In the early journalistic writings about his travels to England (1860) and his rambles through the province of Brandenburg (1862 ff.), he developed that ironic and intelligent precision which served him supremely well in his major novels, *Irrungen, Wirrungen* (1888), *Effi Briest* (1895), and *Der Stechlin* (1898).

Technically, he is the most conspicuous of the leading German novelists of the time. His composition is, in an unromantic sense, picturesque; he enlivens his soberly threaded plots with a pointed anecdote, an epigrammatic turn of phrase, and a surprising detail; his devices of portraiture are never pedantic, but always subtle and gentlemanly. Even though the range of his inventiveness is limited, he creates, by his respect for the significant accidents of life and by his careful use of transparent symbols, masterly accounts of human relationships. If, standing between the middle class and the aristocracy, he was ineffective as a social critic, this failure is due, not to an indifference toward contemporary political issues, but rather to the fact that he was interested almost wholly, and without making the slightest concession to sentimentality, in the behavior of the individual. With all his astonishing skill at analyzing the contemporary world in its frailty, he is not a novelist of ideas; and although it may not be altogether possible to rank Fontane with the best of his English and French contemporaries, he is the only writer of German fiction in the late nineteenth century who could, now and again, have held his own in their company.

No less significant a narrative artist, though of an entirely different temperament, is Wilhelm Raabe (1831–1910). In the originality of his idiom, in the breadth of his vision, and in the warmth of his sympathy, he surpasses, at times, Fontane himself, who has much of the cool detachment of Flaubert, while Raabe continues the fertile tradition of the German baroque imagination. He is one of the few genuine German humorists; but his humor, like his characters and their settings, demands from the reader a sympathetic understanding of the depth and breadth of German provincial life. His work represents the impressive climax of the literature of German bourgeois idealism. With Gotthelf, Stifter, Keller, and Fontane, he is one of the chief novelists of the nineteenth century. A far greater artist than his popular contemporary, Gustav Freytag, and a less self-conscious craftsman than Fontane, he is the most genuine storyteller of his generation. Without being either as subjective or as effusively sentimental as Germany's greatest romantic novelist, "Jean Paul" Richter (1763–1825), he shares Richter's affection for the minutely revealing detail and the bizarre characters of a proudly class-conscious society. His language, like Richter's also, is rich and occasionally overcharged with recondite learning, but inexhaustible in its wealth of invention.

His first novel, written in the form of a chronicle (*Die Chronik der Sperlingsgasse*, published in 1857 under the characteristic pseudonym, "Jacob Corvinus"), is in its subject matter reminiscent of the idyllic and retiring sensibility of the "Biedermeier" decade; he speaks already with the seasoned authority of a wise observer of life, and fixes his particular manner of idealistic realism which he sums up, in *Die Leute aus dem Walde* (1863), in one often-quoted sentence, "Look up to the stars; watch life in the streets"—*Sieh nach den Sternen! Gib acht auf die Gassen!*

If, during his middle years, Raabe found himself in agreement with the gist of Schopenhauer's pessimistic ideas, he was, nevertheless, a positive, yet not uncritical, defender of those threatened cultural values which his gilded age seemed willing to forget. He never advanced to a resolute analysis of the capitalistic situation which was about to develop, nor did the contemporary socialistic and naturalistic ideologies interest him as such. But in his three best known novels, *Der Hungerpastor* (1864), *Abu Telfan* (1867), and *Der Schüdderump* (1870), he foreshadowed the German and European crisis of morals with as much insight and possibly greater wisdom than even Nietzsche himself. All three works, related in substance but not in plot, portray the eventual triumph of inner strength and integrity of feeling over the forces of dissolution. Not unlike the people in the work of his northern German contemporaries, Storm, Reuter, and Groth,

which the romantics had excelled and which was now, in the seventies and eighties, once again the favorite German narrative vehicle. Twenty-four volumes of Paul Heyse's (1830–1914) *Deutscher Novellenschatz* (1871 ff.) testify to the popularity of this attractive genre in which an impressive number of genuine fabulists spoke authoritatively and appealingly. Among these, Keller and his Swiss compatriot, Conrad Ferdinand Meyer (1825–1898), possess the most varied resources. Keller is serene and lambently ironic, and, as a consummate humorist, more effective than any other modern German novelist; his earlier *Leute von Seldwyla* (1856, 1874) his *Züricher Novellen* (1878), and, above all, the exquisite story cycle of *Das Sinngedicht* (1881) represent the richest achievement of the realistic perception. Meyer combines in his more complex disposition instinctive liking for the man of action and an almost quietistic tendency towards contemplation and withdrawal, which lends to his stories (*Jürg Jenatsch,* 1876, *Der Heilige,* 1880, and *Die Versuchung des Pescara,* 1887) a peculiarly dramatic force. Another of the group, Theodor Storm (1817–1888), a northerner, has, in spite of certain sentimental mannerisms and a persistent attachment to nostalgic and pseudo-social themes, remained one of the truly pleasing minor storytellers of the period. His gifts are essentially lyrical and even diffuse, but the discreet reserve of his art has produced psychological portraits of great charm.

In many of these transcendentally realistic narratives—to which might be added the attractive work of the Austrians, Marie von Ebner-Eschenbach (1830–1916) and Ferdinand von Saar (1833–1906)—the provincial themes of German fiction predominate; but the soundness of their form and the quality of their human appeal give to them a vitality and permanence not to be found after the turn of the century. Indeed, compared to the substantial achievements of these five or six conservative prose writers, the naturalistic controversy, which developed at the same time, seems in retrospect little more than a brief formal interlude. But, like the subsequent challenge of the expressionistic point of view, it served as a climactic shock without which the new "modern" idiom of the twentieth century could not have been finally established. This critical skirmish was conducted with vigor and some bitterness mainly in those cities in which the recent European reorganization had vested economic and social strength—in Berlin, Leipzig, and Munich. Some of the new literary journals (Paul Lindau's *Die Gegenwart,* 1872 ff., Julius Rodenberg's *Deutsche Rundschau,* 1874 ff., Michael Georg Conrad's southern *Die Gesellschaft,* 1885 ff., and Otto Brahm's *Freie Bühne für modernes Leben,* 1890 ff.) sustained the controversy between the rear guard of the idealistic tradition and the cosmopolitan advance of the pseudo-scientific and mechanistic-minded forces. In their pages, and in the belligerent pamphlets of the outstanding protagonists, the voices of a new generation were first heard, and a distinguished group of European writers (Ibsen, Zola, Tolstoy, Maupassant, Strindberg, Hamsun, and Hauptmann) now broke into the established world of bourgeois beliefs.

The compelling influence of the mid-century's three most persuasive analysts, Taine, Darwin, and Marx, left the German writers especially preoccupied with the determinist pattern of life. At the beginning of the eighties the fascination of the idealistic tradition appears to be coming to an end: whether optimistic at the prospect of evolutionary progress or resigned to a pessimistic immobility, the artist finds himself compelled to abandon the humanistic faith in the creative will of the individual. At a moment when German imperialism begins its most aggressive career, the work of Schopenhauer seems, paradoxically, to find its belated fulfillment in the naturalistic philosophy.

At the same time the earlier predominance of the provincial and idyllic themes gives way to a more deliberate emphasis upon the social issues of the city, and of those human types and classes that had not yet actually entered the main stream of self-conscious literature. In the flourishing tradition of German popular fiction and poetry the subjects of class conflict and social tension had, of course, not been uncommon. But the use of familiar melodramatic properties, now drawn from areas hitherto treated with condescension, did not necessarily constitute evidence of social awareness.

It can be doubted whether the naturalistic movement as a whole was genuinely alive to the inexorable and radical nature of the economic situation. The marks of social calamity were recorded with much humanitarian concern, but in the main they were presented as the result of human depravity and a temporary aberration from the normal conditions of the bourgeois order. It is true that, by focusing upon the signs of grievous inequality and exploitation, the naturalistic artists created an attitude of curiosity and interest without which much of the later literature of genuine and aggressive cultural criticism could not have been effective. But the fundamental intention of most of these writers was aesthetic, not political. They were absorbed by a laborious interest in form, and their very insistence upon objectivity of transcription reveals the degree of their sophistication. Many of them were, in the face of newly discovered signs of distress, caught between callousness and sentimentality.

Although the self-denying technique of minutely detailed observation and description was not the contribution of the young naturalists alone, the new matter was being set forth with extreme baldness of gesture and design. The writing of the naturalists was, on the whole, without distinction. The instrument of the German language, which had, since the days of

Goethe, become so impressive an organ of thought and eloquence, now failed to serve and discipline the narrative artist. It is today almost impossible not to be shocked by the lack of literary integrity in even the more seriously applauded works of the time. The popularity, for instance, of the prolific novelist and dramatist, Hermann Sudermann (1857–1928), can hardly be explained on the grounds of intrinsic excellence; it was certainly not due to the novelty of his style or the superiority of his vision. In such works as *Frau Sorge* (1887) or *Der Katzensteg* (1889) he merely turned the impartial conscientiousness of Zola or Tolstoy into German sentimentality, and failed to achieve more than a transparently crude artifice. With his uncertain and snobbish temperament Sudermann was not able to make the intellectual and creative decision which is required of the truly effective social novelist. It was only in the admirable but little known *Litauische Geschichten* (1917) that he established a convincing manner of his own.

The reason for the ultimate insufficiency of the German naturalistic writer is not far to seek. It was not only that the somewhat naïve critical belief in the staccato reproduction of a narrow and pathetic segment of life, applied as it was with the stubbornness of their limited talent, proved to be a mere literary device, but the human substance with which the new idiom should have been enlivened was entirely lacking. Moreover, the belief in man's dependence upon the external social condition, arising out of a certain pseudoscientific determinism, obscured their sense of the more radical forces underlying the situation. The absence in the German writers of the powerful human understanding which animated the Russian, French, and English naturalists from Goncharov to George Moore made any fiction of real depth and distinction improbable.

It was in the drama—or the theater—that the nervous manner of meticulous reporting proved to be most legitimate and effective. Fontane, one of the first to recognize the courage and justice of the naturalistic idiom, bestowed his early and generous praise not upon a work of fiction but upon an experimental play, *Die Familie Selicke* (1890) by Arno Holz (1863–1929) and Johannes Schlaf (1862–1941).

The German drama of the immediate past had not been undistinguished. Still bound to the idealistic conventions of belief and technique, its subject matter had (in Hebbel) philosophical substance, (in Grillparzer) patriotic fervor, and, here and there (as in Anzengruber), a quality of genuine popular appeal. But the most remarkable dramatic figure of the age, musician, poet, and cultural critic, was Richard Wagner (1813–1883).

Wagner's contribution to the nineteenth century is difficult to assess. In retrospect his importance seems inexhaustible: his peremptory claim of leadership for the artist, intolerable in any other nation, was in the

German tradition; and with the insight of one whose principal aim it was to be effective as seer and poet, he recognized the waning relevance of all contemporary media of imaginative communication. His choice of mythological subjects was to supply new substance to the dramatic stage, and the extraordinary sensuality of his perception found inevitable expression in the most nervous and personal forms of music that had yet been conceived. With the support of music the diminished pulse of the German poetic language was to recover its traditional strength.

But Wagner's significance is not confined to mere experiments in form, however far-reaching. He was, in the nineteenth century, the most clear-sighted critic of the declining bourgeois life. Yet, unlike Nietzsche, his faith in the regeneration of the Christian middle class remained unshaken, and the tremendous efforts by which he compelled his age to accept his vision of greatness were finally crowned in 1876 when his festival house at Bayreuth was opened with a performance of the *Nibelungen* tetralogy. Six years later *Parsifal,* the most specifically religious of his dramas of redemption, concluded the career of a unique artist whose creative work and critical convictions, with all their one-sidedness, were more widely disturbing than those of any other of his European contemporaries.

The naturalistic drama differed in essential respects, however, from Wagner's romantically conceived and emotionally strenuous notion of the *Gesamtkunstwerk.* With something like pedantic consistency the new playwrights proceeded to dissolve the heroic center of the classical drama into a dull variety of involuntary gestures and episodic situations; even in its subject matter the naturalistic drama, narrowly and literally preoccupied with crime, hunger, and disease, was at first tiresome and monotonous. Only occasionally—for instance in so bristling a comedy of manners as Arno Holz's *Die Sozialaristokraten* (1896)—, and especially in the hands of its most vigorous and gifted artist, Gerhart Hauptmann, it became a telling and flexible form.

Gerhart Hauptmann's (b. 1862) achievement is not easily summarized. In many respects he has been an awkward and, at times, even irresponsible artist whose long career has been filled with surprises and disappointments. But in the company of his more superficial and less courageous—and now generously forgotten—contemporaries, he remains, in Germany, the only genuine representative of the modern realistic drama. The spectacular aspects of his early success, *Vor Sonnenaufgang* (1889) brought him instantaneous prominence. He had, once and for all, shown the dramatic possibilities of a truly "modern" conflict. But within a brief period of ten or fifteen years, he enlarged the indistinct medium of naturalistic speech and action into a variety of impressive poetic accomplishments. The influence upon him of Ibsen's, Björnson's, and Dostoevsky's religious idealism is strong at first, and compassion remains his most persistent trait. *Die Weber* (1892), a stirring account of exploited and tragically charged human beings, has proved to be Hauptmann's most straightforward work, free of the cliché and claptrap of similar propaganda plays. By the force and detachment of his own temperament he develops the naturalistic style both in comedy (*Der Biberpelz,* 1893) and in historical tragedy (*Florian Geyer,* 1895) to such perfection that the nineteenth-century epic drama seems here to attain its final fruition. Two later and equally powerful plays, *Fuhrmann Henschel* (1898) and *Rose Bernd* (1903), reaffirmed his skill in human portraiture; but Hauptmann had then already passed beyond the strict pattern of naturalistic doctrine, for in *Hanneles Himmelfahrt* (1893) and his most widely played lyrical drama in verse, *Die versunkene Glocke* (1896), he had made use of newly developed symbolic poetic devices. With *Und Pippa tanzt* (1906) his dramatic work reached a masterly climax; what followed in the more than fourteen plays to come was reiteration and reassertion of a singularly enterprising but never fully disciplined vitality. It is a sign of the vigorous resources of Hauptmann's talent that, throughout his later career, whether in his plays, his epics (*Till Eulenspiegel,* 1928), or his narrative and autobiographical prose (*Der Narr in Christo Emanuel Quint,* 1910; *Der Ketzer von*

Soana, 1918; *Die Insel der grossen Mutter,* 1925; *Das Abenteuer meiner Jugend,* 1937), he has displayed an astonishing range of technical accomplishments. But what has given him continued relevance among the more recent poets and dramatists is his faith in the creative value of irrational and instinctive energies. He has remained characteristically immune to the disturbing influence of Nietzsche: his strength is drawn not from the philosophers but from a deep sense of the nervous energy and delicate contour of the individual human being.

Hauptmann's work owes much to the flourishing theatrical culture of the time. Three events indicate the memorable advance of the Berlin theater: the production in 1874, by the Duke of Meiningen's troupe, of Shakespeare's *Julius Caesar,* a display of realistic staging and mass scenes which was not to be easily surpassed; the establishment in 1883 of the Deutsches Theater, which, under the directorship of Adolf L'Arronge, was to devote itself both to the classics and to the more drastic new portrayals of Berlin life; and the founding in 1889 of the Verein Freie Bühne. With its first production (Ibsen's *Ghosts*), and by its sensitiveness to the contemporary idiom, it gained at once, under its director, Otto Brahm, the respect and enthusiasm of the younger generation. The work of Max Reinhardt (1873–1943), the most agile theatrical artist of the past fifty years, gave to the newly invigorated medium particular distinction. With an extraordinary feeling for the spectacular elements of the old Austrian baroque theater, he combined a metropolitan instinct for the subtleties of poetic effect, and a flair for the new function of actor and stage designer. His wide range, from Molière to Strindberg, from Gorky's *Night Asylum* to Johann Strauss's *Die Fledermaus,* from Goethe to Georg Kaiser, suggests the measure of his contribution to the vitality and elegance of the stage which for long has been, and is, especially at the present time, the one artistic area within which the collective devotion of the Germans to the symbols and images of art finds conspicuous and valid public expression.

It was, as a matter of fact, the imaginative strength of the new theater which, directly or indirectly, facilitated for the younger writers the transition from the unpromising doctrine of naturalism to more flexible and more specifically poetic forms. Whether the generation of poets, painters, or musicians, which now began to re-examine the sources and aims of the work of art, declared its allegiance to an "impressionist," "symbolist," or "neoromantic" group, its common concern was with the irrational source of the artist's vision. The new poetry did not, of course, at once abandon its preoccupation with the pressing contemporary subject matter of social issues. On the contrary, two of its most forceful representatives, the poets Detlev von Liliencron (1844–1909) and Richard Dehmel (1863–1920), with all their nervous impressionistic perception, were intensely, at times even hectically, concerned with the current issues of sex, social tension, and the city. Those were relevant themes, and the conservative talents assembled in Heyse's *Neues Münchner Dichterbuch* (1882) are the poorer for their want of them. Wilhelm Bölsche in his influential essay *Die naturwissenschaftlichen Grundlagen der Poesie* (1887), the young Arno Holz in his first volume of lyrics, *Das Buch der Zeit* (1885), and the *avant-garde* writers in Arent's *Moderne Dichtercharaktere* (1885) had stressed the link between the poet and the new "scientific" or the "French" manner of seeing the world. And it is true that Taine and Zola exercised, for a time, a perceptible influence upon both novelists and poets. But the stirring example of poetic inspiration and political fervor was Walt Whitman, whose poetry had long been vigorously defended by Freiligrath and was now widely read in K. Knortz and T. W. Rolleston's translation (1889), and energetically recognized by Johannes Schlaf (*Walt Whitman,* 1897, 1904). Against the lean and formalized imagery of the German mid-century poets, Whitman represented the voice and rhythm of unself-conscious imagination.

In Dehmel and Liliencron, in the later poetry of Holz (*Phantasus,* 1898–1899), and in one or two minor impressionist poets, the curiously delicate and on the whole unmartial sensibility of the post-Bismarckian era was to find its appropriate idiom. Their perception was not merely precise and accurate, but subtle; and the pulse of their verse was more passionate and restless than might have appeared tolerable, even to the most understanding poets of the older generation. But, for the first time since the belated flowering of the romantics in the 1820's and 1830's, the poet spoke with the ardor of the genuinely inspired singer. Of the two prominent poets, Liliencron is the more casual and, at times, the more attractive: Byronic verve (*Poggfred*, 1896) is in him combined with a singularly brittle and musical sensitivity; indeed, poet and soldier (*Adjutantenritte*, 1883) seem naturally and effectively in unison. Dehmel's work, on the other hand, is distinguished by a strong metaphysical impulse; indebted to Nietzsche, to his rhythm and imagery more, perhaps, than to the substance of his thinking, Dehmel's poetry (*Aber die Liebe*, 1893; *Weib und Welt*, 1896; *Verwandlungen der Venus*, 1907) rises from the affirmation of pagan abundance and vitality to a genuinely religious attitude of universal love. The physical and the spiritual, "Eros" and "Agape" were in him equally present. With his humanitarian sense of social responsibility, he influenced the working-class poets soon to emerge, whereas his realistic and earth-bound outlook separated him from the dithyrambic effusiveness of the later expressionists.

It is now necessary that a generation of Anti-Alexanders should arise, endowed with the supreme strength necessary for gathering up, binding together, and joining the individual threads of the fabric so as to prevent their being scattered to the four winds. The object is not to cut the Gordian knot of Greek culture after the manner adopted by Alexander, and then to leave its frayed ends fluttering in all directions; it is rather to bind it after it has been loosed. That is our task to-day.

NIETZSCHE

II

THE ANTI-ALEXANDERS

THE YEAR 1890 indicates the beginning of a far-reaching imaginative movement, of which Hugo von Hofmannsthal, Rainer Maria Rilke, and Stefan George are the most striking representatives. About George's extraordinary and masterly personality gathered the proud apostles of the aristocratic and anti-materialistic faith, who, in the *Blätter für die Kunst* (1892 ff.), denounced the pedestrian dullness of naturalism. Hofmannsthal was bound to the new attitude, if not directly at least indirectly, by the patrician delicacy and depth of his intelligence. Rilke, the sensitive easterner, the *pater seraphicus,* kept cautiously apart from the slowly forming circle of George's followers. But all three, throughout their work, are concerned with the question of the poet's position in an antipoetical world.

In the lyrical poetry at the turn of the century a feeling of the artist's self-consciousness is especially obvious. To the young Nietzsche (1844–1900), who had met Wagner in 1868, it was axiomatic that civilization and culture should culminate in the artist; with him in 1872 (*Die Geburt der Tragödie*), as it had also been with Schopenhauer, no creative activity transcended that of the musician. But the poetry of the nineties, whether it came from the East, West, or South, suggested a more cautious view of the artist; it reflected the precarious situation of the man of feeling and vision, in a society which was absorbed in less sensitive pursuits and in which thoughtful observers recognized an ever-widening discrepancy between action and imagination. The Kaiser's refusal to patronize the naturalistic playwrights was merely obtuse, the overwhelming public embarrassment in the face of Baudelaire, Wedekind, or Strindberg was more serious. The word *décadence,* which was to become so symptomatic of the intellectual climate of the nineties, meant, of course, more than degeneracy and moral degradation; it conveyed the pathetic increase of spiritual and nervous energies at the expense of a more direct display of biological strength and bourgeois efficacy. Thomas Mann's *Buddenbrooks* (1901), a prodigiously gifted young man's first novel, is a paraphrase upon this theme, and his tales, from *Der kleine Herr Friedemann* (1898) and the entertainingly moralizing *Königliche Hoheit* (1909) to *Der Tod in Venedig* (1913), reflect with singular perspicacity some of the spiritual elements which now motivate the young neoromantics: a lively sense of the irrational heritage of the German past, an insistence upon the traditional responsibility of the man of letters, and the deepening concern with the virtues and destiny of man.

These were, of course, in substance questions which Nietzsche had raised; and it is perhaps no exaggeration to say that Nietzsche's work is the gigantic gauge by which not only those under his immediate influence, but also each generation since his death in 1900, have measured their world.

In one respect Nietzsche belongs to the tradition of the French moralists: he is not so much a systematic philosopher as, rather, an uncompromising social and cultural critic who illuminates the condition of man in a variety of directions and by a brilliant use of aphoristic forms. Like Montaigne and Pascal, La Rochefoucauld, Vauvenargues, and Stendhal, he describes, analyzes, questions, and attacks the past and present concepts of human existence. While his targets, however specific at times, may seem to shift, they can be found in the main within three areas: the tradition of European rationalism, the scientific materialism of the nineteenth century, and the inherited concepts of the idealistic and Christian philosophies. His inquiry into these issues is as categorical as it is prophetic; and his challenges, whether in the lithe prose of his earlier works (*Unzeitgemässe Betrachtungen*, 1873, *Menschliches, Allzumenschliches*, 1878, and *Also Sprach Zarathustra*, 1883–1885) or in the demonic and nihilistic pages of the later writings (*Jenseits von Gut und Böse*, 1886, *Zur Genealogie der Moral*, 1887, and *Ecce Homo*, 1888), cut straight into the center of all bourgeois values.

Like Karl Marx, Nietzsche insists upon the ideological, the "perspectival" nature of all moral judgments; but, as if anticipating the immeasurable crisis of our own time, he contends (in *Der Wille zur Macht*, 1888) that "the question of values is more fundamental than the problem of certainty." In the reassessment of the tenets by which the contemporary world is being sustained, he formulates the task of all those who have faced his acid questions. The countervalues by which he would transform the present situation of man are stated in hyperbolical and often puzzling images; the will to power, immoralism, the superman, and eternal recurrence merely indicate the kind and range of his envisioned table of values, and nothing would be a more unjust perversion of Nietzsche's original philosophical intention than to regard these oft-mistaken notions literally. Nietzsche's work is inexhaustible and, by the fullness and variety of suggestive detail, it has offered itself, as one recent critic has wittily put it, equally to the "gentle" and the "tough" among his followers. Formulated in what is perhaps the most resilient language of the century, his peremptory judgments are ultimately directed at the whole nature of man, at the biological source of his perception, the depth and fiber of his emotional and intellectual constitution, and, above all, his moral obligation to a society which finds itself in a precarious state of crisis. Whatever the value of Nietzsche's contribution to particular cultural issues may be, the very absence in his work of clear-cut and positive answers to his own questions compelled those who found his inquiries relevant to search for solutions and definitions. In effect, Nietzsche acted as a catalyst who caused change and reaction in others, without himself being, in every case, willing or capable of providing a plausible answer.

For the literary artist, both in Germany and elsewhere in Europe, the impact of Nietzsche's work was bound to be of the greatest significance. It was not his poetry which proved to be of consequence; for although he chose for his *Zarathustra* a highly charged dithyrambic manner, he was not primarily a poet. Nietzsche's poems are the expression of an extraordinarily sensitive and musical mind with a fine, though not unconventional, talent for brief and succinct poetic forms. They are carried by the same force of flashing and translucent insight which illuminates his prose. But Nietzsche's influence upon succeeding artists sprang from his general philosophical attitude rather than from the nature of his literary idiom. Impressionists, symbolists, and expressionists alike found themselves, each in a different way, supported by the great questioner.

Among the early impressionists, those who were indebted to the brothers Goncourt and the French painters from Monet to Renoir, the preoccupation was, clearly, with a new understanding of the artist's private sensibility. If the figure and function of the artist in society was soon to become the central issue of much of the new writing, the particular nature of the poet's human disposition and his mode of apprehending the world led to speculations of a far-reaching kind. In Germany, Eduard von Hartmann (1842–1906), the philosopher of the "unconscious," had some time before (1869) dissolved the round individuality of the ego into a series of atomic and fleeting perceptions which were, in the subsequent distinguished psychological studies of Mach, Wundt, and Freud, and especially in the intuitive and metaphysical philosophy of Bergson, confirmed as the new units of experience. The symbols of Baudelaire and Mallarmé, the light gestures of Liebermann, and the "small sensations" of Cézanne and Debussy make up some of the most generally distinctive elements of the intellectual climate of the European *fin de siècle*.

Vienna, always delicate and melancholy in its temper, provided in fact and imagery the suitable setting for the new writing: the emotional refinements of Arthur Schnitzler (1862–1931) were appropriately projected against the background of this city and its society. His early plays and the muffled short stories of the twenties, with their easy dialogue and tenuous action, will remain symptomatic of a listless age. The caste-bound officers and the warmhearted, lightheaded women of his world, caught in the enchantment of a momentary happiness, seem never seriously disturbed. They are aware of the transitoriness of life, but more naïvely preoccupied with the melody of death than the weary Claudio in Hofmannsthal's *Der Tor und der Tod*. The sense of loneliness, which was, in the novels of Kafka or the mature elegies of Rilke, to become the source of deep despair, is here lightly conveyed in melancholy half-tone and the indistinctness of a nostalgic dream.

But the element of impressionistic frailty is not the only quality of the Viennese generation at the turn of the century. The Socratic sketches of Peter Altenberg (1859–1919; *Wie ich es sehe*, 1896, *Neues Altes*, 1911, *Mein Lebensabend*, 1919) suggest a characteristic type of "sophisticated" enthusiasm. In Richard Beer-Hofmann (b. 1866) and Richard von Schaukal (b. 1874), a pronounced gift for form and a creative allegiance to the European tradition have produced a conservative poetry which has remained alive and important. Schaukal is of the two the more versatile and flexible; his early *Verse* (1896) was followed by a series of competent volumes in poetry and prose, both lyrical and reflective (*Das Buch der Seele*, 1908, *Gezeiten der Seele*, 1926, *Essays*, 1925, and *Erkenntnisse und Betrachtungen*, 1934), with which he reaches beyond the subsequent fluctuations of literary taste into the present, when his work seems once again to have assumed a certain technical relevance. Beer-Hofmann's *Graf von Charolais* (1905) is the outstanding neoromantic drama of the time; his later dramatic poems, especially *Jaâkobs Traum* (1918) and *Der junge David* (1934), generously conceived and carefully figured, show the lively concurrence of inspiration and reserve which is the result not only of his deep and splendid Jewish vision, but of his affinity to a conception of the poet's imaginative function and responsibility which George and Hofmannsthal were to represent so impressively.

Hugo von Hofmannsthal (1874–1929) is the most conspicuous of the Viennese poets of the nineties. He developed the resources of his Austrian heritage into a body of disciplined verse and prose so distinguished that his lyrical dramas (*Gestern,* 1891, *Der Tod des Tizian,* 1892, and *Der Tor und der Tod,* 1893) and his early "impressionistic" poetry (*Gesammelte Gedichte,* 1907) were but the promising beginning of a literary career which continued and strengthened the spiritual tradition of the great French, English, and German poets—especially Keats and Hölderlin—and surpassed in variety, breadth, and wisdom that of any of his contemporaries. In spite of his early but never uncritical attachment to the neoromantic writers of the time, to Pater and Wilde, Barrès, Mallarmé, and D'Annunzio, he fashioned his substance in a direction essentially different from theirs. Sensitiveness to the rich melody and a delight in the spacious gestures of the southern baroque remained important sources of his dramatic imagination; indeed, music and the theater were to him media essentially related to his own poetic intention: in Richard Strauss (*Der Rosenkavalier,* 1911) and Max Reinhardt he found perceptive and, in some measure, congenial collaborators. But to repeat the hackneyed objection to Hofmannsthal's "aestheticism" is to disregard the main body of his mature work. In one of his most memorable essays (*Brief des Lord Chandos,* 1901), he himself suggests the deceptive weakness in the impressionist position: in the disguise of a farseeing Elizabethan courtier-poet, but with obvious reference to his own generation, he confesses to a paralyzing failure of courage in the face of the overwhelming experience of death. From this point of inner crisis, Hofmannsthal henceforth moves towards an attitude in which life and death seem to become mutually significant and in which the constant shadow or the sudden vision of death produce that creative moral challenge without which man will not survive.

In some of the works of the years before and during the First World War, in *Elektra* (1903), in the much-praised and effective adaptation of the old *Everyman* morality play (1911), in *Ariadne auf Naxos* (1912), but particularly in the allusive and complex fairy tale, *Die Frau ohne Schatten* (1919), the progress of human endeavor from self-centeredness and irresponsibility to the efficacy of moral resolve and judgment is presented in poetry of genuine splendor and force. Still more strikingly he insists, in *Das Salzburger Grosse Welttheater* (1922), upon the scope as well as the limitation of the human achievement, its coherence in forms of social and religious traditions, and the hierarchical pattern of its immutable order.

His last play, *Der Turm* (final version, 1925), points most clearly to the moving interrelation, in Hofmannsthal's work, of contemporary concerns and perennial convictions. It is the crowning achievement of a remarkable life. Like Rilke's late *Elegien,* it is charged—even, perhaps, overcharged—with extraordinary spiritual relationships. From the chaos, murder, and disorder of the world, there arises in this tragedy the saintlike figure of a heroic human being who, by the compelling strength of his integrity and by his absolute devotion to the virtues of self-denial, sacrifice, and faith, re-establishes the broken values of the age.

In the company of Rilke and George, Hofmannsthal will remain the greatest, not because of his superior private sensibility or any revolutionary or formal contribution to a new poetic idiom, nor because of an attitude of militant disagreement with the practices of contemporary living, but because in him and his work, as possibly in no other European poet of this time, the living impulse and example of an effective spiritual and moral humanism are magnificently realized.

Yet it should not be thought that Hofmannsthal's work shares, in any superficial sense, in the fashionable return to medieval concepts. No one could have been less recondite and more aware of the common and pressing problems of the day. In an astonishing body of inspired critical essays, addresses, and reflections (*Die Prosaischen Schriften gesammelt*, 1907, 1917, 3 vols.), he turns his attention upon all aspects of the contemporary experience: his rich, measured, and illuminated prose is almost unrivaled in German literature. Far from being anxious to enter into the partisan discussion of ephemeral political issues, he appealed at times in the most solemn manner to the sense of European obligation among his Austrian and German compatriots. Especially in the famous address of 1927, *Das Schrifttum als geistiger Raum der Nation*, in which he discusses the spiritual function of literature in national life, he evoked before the Munich students the significant features of an imminent "conservative revolution," a term which he coined and which has since assumed a peculiarly challenging connotation.

If the gravity of tradition and cultural responsibility dominate Hofmannsthal's work, it is the religious crisis of the age which gives direction and significance to the poetry of Rainer Maria Rilke (1875–1926). By temperament and inclination outside of the current naturalistic and impressionistic tendencies, he revealed, in two early collections of poetry, little original strength beyond a sentimental attachment to his native city, Prague, and a lively though undisciplined sensitiveness to certain aesthetic experiences. In his first work he had not yet brought himself to the intensity of devotion or, above all, the sharpness of specific observation that became the conspicuous quality of his later poetry. With *Traumgekrönt* (1897), *Advent* (1898), and *Mir zu Feier* (1899), Rilke began to move towards a more and more depersonalized idiom. The first part of the *Stunden-Buch,* written in 1899 and published in 1905, together with *Von der Pilgerschaft* and *Von der Armuth und vom Tode,* intensifies the impression of an imagination stirred but sometimes clouded by religious fervor.

From 1899 on, he wandered restlessly from one country to another; he traveled in Russia, learned Russian, and on two occasions (in 1899 and 1900) visited Tolstoy. Overwhelmed by the eastern landscape, he crystallized his discovery of the immeasurable presence of God in his graceful *Geschichten vom lieben Gott* (1900, 1904). He seemed at home in all parts of Europe; whether in Paris or Munich, Scandinavia, Spain, Italy, or Switzerland, he developed and deepened everywhere his characteristic sense of space and physical reality. For two years he lived in the painters' colony near Worpswede, where, determined to rid his poetry of all narrative or merely lyrical elements, he wrote most of the poems that were, in 1902, published under the characteristic title, *Das Buch der Bilder* (2d enlarged ed., 1906). Superbly skillful though most of this work has seemed to some, to Rilke it still lacked that firmness of distinct bodies in space in which he felt most palpably the presence of a moving God.

His association in Paris with the great French sculptor Rodin represents perhaps the most significant turn in his poetic career. He had always found himself in sympathy with much of French culture, and had translated Maurice de Guérin, André Gide, and Paul Valéry; but Rodin (like the equally influential Cézanne) became to him a symbol not so much of the French character in general as, rather, of a hard-working craftsman grappling with the completely significant world of tangible objects. The artist's work, Rodin insisted, is the only satisfactory mode of religious activity. Much of Rilke's happy recognition of this attitude entered into his account of the master (*Auguste Rodin,* 1903, 1913). But the two volumes of *Neue Gedichte* (1907, 1908) show the turn in Rilke's conception of the artist even more clearly: they contain his first substantial poetry. In these poems he develops a peculiarly objective form which is not far removed from what was later to be recognized as "pure" poetry, and for which, in Rilke's case, the term *Dinggedicht* has offered itself. He advances now from his earlier private and impressionistic aestheticism to an integration and transformation of his vision into more impersonal symbols. At the same time the poems in *Neue Gedichte* represent, together with the delicate and melancholy prose of his only major narrative, *Die Aufzeichnungen des Malte Laurids Brigge* (1910), the last work in which his impressions, however sublimated and embodied, supplied the material for and the aim of his poetry.

From then on, his life and his poetry began to change. His fame increased rapidly; an earlier book, *Die Weise von Liebe und Tod des Cornets Christoph Rilke* (1906), gained, partly because of its melodramatic and sentimental defects, enormous popularity. A singularly extensive and self-conscious correspondence kept him in touch with a large circle of friends (cf. *Briefe,* 1929 ff.). But in spite of all outward encouragement there followed years of profound despair, frustration, and helplessness. In August, 1914, for once inspired by a feeling of solidarity with his countrymen, he passed through a brief period of exaltation and wrote, in the ecstatic style of Hölderlin's last poems, *Fünf Gesänge*. But this elation did not last. As early as the winter of 1911–1912, he had begun at the castle of Duino in Istria a series of elegies which he seemed unable to complete until, in an extraordinary burst of inspiration, he finished the last of the ten poems in 1922 at Castle Muzot in the Swiss Canton of Valais. These *Duineser Elegien* (1923) Rilke regarded as his supreme achievement; they are, at the same time, the most impressive sequence of great poetry in modern European literature. Their theme is man's, and particularly the poet's, struggle for clarity and coherence; with two exceptions they were written in a rhythmically dithyrambic vers libre, and even though they are charged with elements of philosophical reflection, they demand of the reader above all something of the creative and nervous sensibility which sustained the poet himself. The *Elegien* are the evidence of an overwhelming religious crisis, but with their recurrent emphasis upon the alternation of struggle, death, and regeneration, they represent only one aspect of Rilke's vision. The other, his sense of joy, affirmation, and praise, is the keynote of *Die Sonette an Orpheus* (1923), a series of fifty-five brilliant and exuberantly positive "songs," written in the state of astonishing inspiration in which he finished the last of the *Elegien*. With these two incomparable statements of the cosmic experience, progress, and achievement of the poet, Rilke ended a creative career which is as rare in recent times as it is difficult to appreciate.

It may be that one of the major sources of Rilke's perception was private and romantic; but in an age which is characterized by a disturbing variety of ever-shifting attitudes and concerns, his total contribution is both unique and convincing. We should be unjust if we were to object that his poetry is never, except by profound implication, political; neither in his magnificent late work nor in his correspondence is there evidence of any concern for the simpler and institutional social ties that hold men together. Even the events of the First World War drove Rilke only into a more intense search for the stable realities in which the supremely conscious man, the poet, could find his place.

To contrast him, as has often been done, with his great German contemporary, Stefan George, is merely to stress the peculiarly personal nature of his imagination. Unlike the rigidly stylized and monumental George, Rilke is, ultimately, a sensitive and, at his best, genuinely realistic poet, who succeeded gradually in finding the symbols of a modern religious eloquence. It is, perhaps, not altogether just to dismiss most of his work before the *Neue Gedichte* as unoriginal and dangerously subjective. But it is true that many even of the more popular poems in the *Stundenbuch* and the *Buch der Bilder* lack authority. Rilke was, undoubtedly, an artist whose perception and intensity of application were, throughout most of his life, greater than his powers of resolute mastery. It is difficult in some of his earlier poems to escape a feeling of facility and unmerited ease of mystical intuition. The characteristic poetic figure of the Angel, for instance, on which he frequently focuses and through which he realizes the strength of his overpowering inspiration, occurs even in his early work. But it is not until after the years of complete despondency that the symbol of the Angel emerges, in the severe and peremptory images of the *Elegien,* as the absolute of vision and completeness. Within the allegorical world of a modern paradise, in which, innocently close to the animals, Rilke seeks his way, there is no immediate contact with God, but the Angel appears to the "seraphic" poet as does God to the medieval saint. To approach this source of terrible strength is a task almost too great for man; in children, lovers, and heroes Rilke felt it present, and of them the *Elegien* say much. But the cardinal theme of the *Elegien,* especially of the superb fifth, is not supernatural; it is the precariousness of human life. If, as the cycle draws to a close, the sense of inadequacy gives way to one of trust and strength, it is through the poet's transmutation of what is merely seen or "blindly" lived into a vision of experience, and the acceptance of Death as the final transformer. Grief for the dead was probably for Rilke the most moving human experience (cf. the *Requiem* poems, 1909). In the *Elegien,* therefore, death resolves the discrepancies of man's life. In the subsequent *Sonette an Orpheus* Rilke presents the complement of this vision: here the poet's jubilant song serves to transform even the mutability of life into the permanence of absolute creation.

In George (1868–1933), the third of the great modern German poets, the paradoxical tensions that sustain the pattern of the past fifty years become most sharply visible. His work is not extensive in volume, but in its hard formal deliberateness it is as challenging as that of any poet in modern literature. Like Hofmannsthal, he moved steadily from the resplendent symbolist imagery of his earlier work (*Hymnen, Pilgerfahrten, Algabal,* 1890–1892, *Das Jahr der Seele,* 1897, and *Der Teppich des Lebens,* 1899) to a severer attitude of public poetic responsibility. His inspiration was at every stage of his development disciplined by his cautious intellect, and the high seriousness of his later collections (*Der Siebente Ring,* 1907, *Der Stern des Bundes,* 1914, and *Das Neue Reich,* 1928) reflects a rigorous devotion to an esoteric ideal of spiritual perfection. Between 1907 and 1933 he published only two collections of poetry, but in them he asserts categorically the legislative function of the poet and demands for him a cardinal place within the envisaged fellowship of the "Reich."

George began as the self-appointed center of a small circle of antipositivist minds; he ended not only as a poet who had achieved an extraordinary manner of his own, but as a prophet of national resurgence. These two aspects of his work cannot be separated; indeed, they are, throughout his later career, subtly held together. He is at all times the master and the oracular seer, and as such he belongs in the immediate succession of Nietzsche; aristocratic and aloof, but never divorced from the deep current of the common historical heritage—on the contrary, intensely aware of the cultural and traditional duties of the poet—he achieves the extreme of the deliberate, even heroic, gesture. But George's peremptory manner and the exclusiveness of his nationalistic vision should not lead us to forget that ultimately he represents an attitude of civilized, even overrefined, sensitiveness, rather than a dubious faith in irrational or bluntly racial forces. His magnificent translations of Baudelaire, Swinburne, Mallarmé, Rimbaud, Shakespeare, and Dante reveal the measure of his own spiritual indebtedness, and his allegiance to European culture as a whole. When George's contribution to the greatness and perversity of German life between the wars is properly assessed, it will be found to spring from an insistence upon the primacy of devotion to rare greatness over what he would have considered a looser form of "relativistic" understanding; to the creative strength of hierarchical obedience over sentimental individualism; and to discipline and faith over the claims of private intelligence.

The *Blätter für die Kunst* (1892–1919), at first confined to an exclusive and carefully chosen circle, provided a guarded platform not only for George himself, but for such men as Ludwig Klages (b. 1872), Karl Wolfskehl (b. 1869), and Friedrich Wolters (1876–1930), who have since become conspicuous representatives of the new historical sensibility. The rediscovery of "Jean Paul" Richter and the enthusiastic revival of Hölderlin owe much to the circle. With others of the disciples, George's image of past greatness became the source of a highly perceptive and exalted form of mythography: Gundolf's well-known *Goethe* (1916), Bertram's *Nietzsche* (1918), and such suggestive works as Ernst Kantorowicz's *Kaiser Friedrich II* (1927) and Kurt Hildebrandt's *Platon* (1933) represent the finest reflection of George's vision. For among the poets of the group only two or three have attained distinct significance: Max Dauthendey (1867–1918), an early associate, soon developed his own highly flavored and mystical impressionism; Henry von Heiseler (1875–1928, *Die drei Engel,* 1926, *Legenden der Seele,* 1933, and *Gesammelte Werke,* 1937–1938) and Ernst Bertram (b. 1884, *Der Rhein,* 1922, *Das Nornenbuch,* 1925, and *Wartburg,* 1933), thoughtful and civilized in their manner, have transposed certain of the master's themes into a minor key.

George is, of course, in Germany, no isolated figure. But among the antirationalistic, antimaterialistic spokesmen of the time, he is the most rigorous instance of the contemporary desire to restore certain emotional and intellectual resources to their proper function, to fuse, as Nietzsche had demanded, *Leib, Geist,* and *Seele,* those peculiarly German concepts, once again into a single organ of judgment. And in this concern George was not alone. The distinction which the philosopher and historian, Wilhelm Dilthey (1833–1911), had established between the validity of the natural sciences and the humanistic concepts of the *Geisteswissenschaften* began to affect all aspects of cultural thinking. Both the relativism of the natural sciences (Haeckel, Bölsche) and the conciliatory perspectivism of the "historical school" had gradually given way to modes of understanding which were carefully and profoundly tuned to all the areas of human experience.

The German bent for lively philosophical interpretation was perhaps at no time more effective than during the past forty years when sociological, aesthetic, religious, and historical phenomena were seized upon, at once with the thoroughness of scholarly responsibility and the brilliance of sensitive speculation. Men like Windelband and Lamprecht, Simmel and Husserl, Max Weber, Troeltsch, and Wölfflin systematically gave to the mass of inherited knowledge a vigorous contemporary meaning. Among the literary historians and critics, both within and outside the universities, fresh approaches to the work of art promised a mobilization of the vast store of biographical and textual material which the preceding generation had carefully gathered together. By an unparalleled variety of methods, certain periods—the Renaissance (Burdach), the seventeenth century (Viëtor), and especially the incomparable and double-faced age of Goethe (Walzel, Gundolf, Strich, and Korff) were placed in a new light; critical notions of a more strictly aesthetic nature (e.g., Walzel's *Gehalt und Gestalt*, 1925) were being established, and the principles of a specific *Literaturwissenschaft* were more solidly founded (Ermatinger, Petersen, and Petsch). Related sciences shared in this discussion, and psychological, sociological (Schücking), and ethnological investigations (Nadler) brought the work of art into intellectual contexts from which it had at times been all too carefully excluded.

BEAUTIFUL is resolution. But the really fruitful, the productive, and hence the artistic principle is that which we call reserve. In the sphere of music we love it as the prolonged note, the teasing melancholy of the not-yet, the inward hesitation of the soul, which bears within itself fulfilment, resolution, and harmony, but denies it for a space, withholds and delays, scruples exquisitely yet a little longer to make the final surrender. In the intellectual sphere we love it as irony; that irony which glances at both sides, which plays slyly and irresponsibly—yet not without benevolence—among opposites, and is in no great haste to take sides and come to decisions; guided as it is by the surmise that in great matters, in matters of humanity, every decision may prove premature; that the real goal to reach is not decision, but harmony, accord. And harmony, in a matter of eternal contraries, may lie in infinity; yet that playful reserve called irony carries it within itself, as the sustained note carries the resolution.

THOMAS MANN

III

IRONY AND RESOLUTION

THE dominant intellectual currents among the creative writers of the Wilhelmian era are not easily sifted, but in a comprehensive sense they can be called "political," for all impulses of the time seemed to spring from a deep-rooted sense of unprecedented change in the outer and inner life of the nation. To divide these political convictions, wherever they may occur, into liberal and conservative is perhaps to give unwarranted unity to a large variety of revolutionary attitudes; they are all, at any rate, critical of the bourgeois tenets. The cultural concern and the aggressive terminology of the more distinctly political figures are no less Nietzschean in origin than, on the aesthetic side, the privately poetic temper of the impressionist and symbolist poets. Everywhere, at the turn of the century, a sense of crisis became apparent; the aftermath of 1870 began to merge into a premonition of 1914.

In a casual but nevertheless significant manner, some

of the forces of political dissent can be recognized in the militant satirical weeklies. The South German satirists, with their mocking but prudent strength, were especially effective in the vigor of their comments upon all forms of cultural hypocrisy. *Jugend* and *Simplizissimus,* two of the wittiest of the semipolitical papers, both founded in Munich in 1896, provide genuine and biting social criticism; Karl Kraus (1874–1936, later the editor of the most individualistic organ of Austrian cultural pessimism, *Die Fackel,* 1899 ff.) and the belligerent but securely rooted Bavarian, Ludwig Thoma (1867–1921), were early contributors.

In the North the most conspicuous figure for the next twenty years is Paul Ernst (1866–1933). Socialist in politics but conservative in temperament and neoclassicist in form, he analyzed with real conviction, in his extensive and varied writings, the collapse of German idealism (*Zusammenbruch des deutschen Idealismus,* 1918). Nietzsche's influence upon his thinking is in many respects unmistakable. With ceaseless energy of thought and severe self-discipline, he challenged, in his austere tragedies (*Canossa,* 1908, *Brunhild,* 1909, and *Ariadne auf Naxos,* 1912), as well as in many expert narrative works (*Der schmale Weg zum Glück,* 1904, *Saat auf Hoffnung,* 1916, *Komödiantengeschichten,* 1920, *Geschichten aus dem Süden,* 1925, and others), the determinism and fatalism of the naturalistic doctrines. A number of mature critical studies (e.g., *Der Weg zur Form,* 1906, and *Ein Credo,* 1912) demonstrate his fine sense for the qualities of craftsmanship in the various European literatures, which he never failed to contrast and relate fruitfully to the creative energies of his own German tradition. But as essayist and man of letters Paul Ernst never confined himself to the aesthetic issue; if his "classicist" characteristics are stressed, it is only to emphasize the fact that he conceived of the literary life in broadly political terms. The work of the poet, that is, seemed to him —and, indeed, to many others—to have meaning only in so far as it established ideals of social consequence. In a period of widespread dissolution of values so one-sided an attitude, no matter how vigorously and sensibly advanced, could not fail to appear out of tune with the prevailing analytical temper. But it is an attitude which has its striking parallels elsewhere in Europe and which culminates, in Germany, in the figures of Nietzsche and Stefan George.

Perhaps no part of the literary life profited more from the seriousness with which the place of the arts was now being discussed than German fiction at the turn of the century. The refinement of perception and the probing deftness which gave such delicacy to the poets now added range and effectiveness to the work of the novelist. It has often been observed that a firm social background might, in the nineteenth century, have produced a more realistic and less self-conscious type of national fiction, but this defect, it seemed, was now being turned into a virtue; for the world, however disjointed, was to be portrayed in the most private and sceptical manner.

Even though the new novel is, therefore, highly individualistic, it reflects, nevertheless, the strong interest of the time in matters of a broader cultural kind; impatience with the stale conventions of living and, at the same time, willingness to recognize the importance of compelling intellectual traditions provide the characteristic double impulse of the more sensitive novelists. In the distinguished writings of Eduard von Keyserling (1855–1918), for instance, the paralysis of will and feeling among the old Baltic aristocracy is rendered with a suggestiveness and understatement reminiscent of Fontane. And among the women writers of the period (Isolde Kurz, b. 1853, Helene Voigt-Diederichs, b. 1875, Clara Viebig, b. 1860) the combination of psychological insight and adherence to weighty inherited attitudes can be well observed. Not many of them attain the intelligence and brilliance of expression of Ricarda Huch (b. 1864), whose patrician novels, *Erinnerungen von Ludolf Ursleu dem Jüngeren* (1893) and *Vita somnium breve* (1903), were followed by a series of broad historical works in which scholarly solidity and expertness of narrative style are happily combined. The refinement of her analytical talent is never, even in her lighter fiction (*Der Fall Deruga,* 1917), without conscience, and in her maturest products, from *Aus der Triumphgasse* (1902) to the recent novel, *Weisse Nächte* (1943), she restrains her neoromantic disposition and creates disciplined works of careful and effective design. The sense of obligating tradition, so pronounced in Ricarda Huch (see her portrait studies of the German romantic age, *Die Romantik,* 1899 ff., and the critical essays on certain artists to whom she is mainly indebted—Meyer, Böcklin, and Keller) is at the same time one of the dominant traits of the period itself. By turning not merely to the forms but the convictions of the past, many of the impressionist novelists and poets succeeded in giving permanence to their work.

Almost wholly outside the more fashionable literary practices of the time stands the Swiss poet and novelist, Carl Spitteler (1845–1924). When, in 1919, the Nobel Prize was awarded to him, it was not only in recognition of the masterly, realistic novels, *Conrad der Leutenant* (1898), *Imago* (1906), and the enchanting tale, *Die Mädchenfeinde* (1907), but also of the two epic poems, *Der Olympische Frühling* (1900–1906, revised, 1909) and *Prometheus und Epimetheus* (1881). While the one, in its magnificent blending of mythological substance and a creative use of beautiful speech and rhythm, suggests the richness of Spitteler's power of figuration, the other, especially in its later version, *Prometheus der Dulder* (1924), stresses the moral and cultural values which contribute not merely to individual satisfaction but to the strengthening of the social order.

This, of course, is the issue with which the three or four most distinguished German poets of the new century were to be profoundly concerned, and which can, among the writers of fiction, be recognized most explicitly in the work of Thomas Mann (b. 1875).

In no other figure of the past hundred years are personal gifts and regional characteristics, elements of tradition as well as cautious liberalism, nationalist and cosmopolitan features, so happily and strikingly fused to produce a lasting and representative German achievement. In Thomas Mann's novels the formal detachment of Flaubert and Fontane now merges expressly and tangibly with the emotional temper of the German romantic heritage. The propitious circumstances of his birth in the old and bourgeois Hanseatic city of Lübeck, the son of a wealthy grain merchant and his wife of South American extraction, have often and rightly been emphasized; and the turns and patterns of his life have served in a curiously fitting manner as the appropriate foil for a remarkable career. After his father's death the family moved to Munich, where Thomas wrote his early short stories ("Gefallen," 1894, *Der kleine Herr Friedemann*, 1898, and others). During a stay in Rome with his elder brother, Heinrich, he began his first novel, *Buddenbrooks* (1901), which was conceived on a small scale as merely a "protracted five-finger exercise with no ulterior advantages," but which developed into a broad account of the history of a Hanseatic family whose strength and prosperity are gradually being undermined by the disintegrating fascination which the arts, Wagner's music, and Schopenhauer's ideas exercise upon its successive generations. J. P. Jacobsen, Turgenieff, and Maupassant are some of the formal models of this brilliant naturalistic novel. Its central theme is the emerging relationship between the bourgeois life of the nineteenth century and the precarious modern sensibility of the artistic temperament. This is, of course, the problem which concerned Thomas Mann throughout his earlier work, especially in his verse drama, *Fiorenza* (1906), and in his three superb short stories, "Tonio Kröger" (1903), "Bekenntnisse des Hochstaplers Felix Krull" (1911, enlarged 1937), and *Der Tod in Venedig* (1913); the first tale "dearest to my heart," the second, suggested by the memoirs of Manolescu, "the best and happiest thing I have done," and the third, one of the most perfect and widely admired *petits romans* written in our time. *Königliche Hoheit* (1909), "a comedy in the form of a novel," has a similar theme. Its artistically minded, aristocratic hero, preoccupied with his private problems, eventually works out his salvation within the social framework of duty and sacrifice instead of becoming a victim of life.

The years during and after the First World War drew Mann, whose tastes and cultural tradition, as he himself insists, were "moral and metaphysical, not political and social," into an ever greater concern with the issues of the day. A long essay, "Friedrich und die grosse Koalition" (1915), and the volume, *Betrachtungen eines Unpolitischen* (1918), represent his "war service with the weapon of thought" and the substance of his conservative political speculations during the European conflict. Especially in the essay "Concerning Virtue" ("Von der Tugend"), he deplores the political ineptitude of German writers, and in this and subsequent pleas (*Von deutscher Republik*, 1923) he calls for a genuine mobilization of the German intellectuals in support of the new state.

In 1924 appeared *Der Zauberberg*, perhaps the most spectacular modern novel of ideas, which was begun as early as 1912 during a three weeks' visit to Davos. The minutely detailed canvas of this characteristically German *Bildungsroman* catches the spiritual pattern of European civilization during the first part of the present century, and projects it into the rarefied atmosphere of a Swiss sanatorium. There, drawn into many baffling relationships, a youthfully innocent and impressionable German engineer, Hans Castorp, discovers the problematical nature of life and death. He observes the puzzling extravagances of an amoral and radically suspended group of individuals, seems even to yield to the fascination of a life without specific weight, but finally, forced into an extreme spiritual crisis, frees himself from the paralyzing temptation of irrational reasoning. "For the sake of goodness and love," he concludes in the cardinal chapter, "man must let death have no sovereignty over his thoughts." The breadth of its intelligence, the subtlety of its arguments, the almost wearying precision of observation, and the consummate craftsmanship of its composition have made *Der Zauberberg* one of the most conspicuous German contributions to the modern European novel.

Work on *Der Zauberberg* was accompanied by the publication of a delightful prose idyll, *Herr und Hund* (1919), and the writing of several volumes of critical essays (*Rede und Antwort,* 1922, *Bemühungen,* 1925, and others), which were followed by later collections of critical prose (*Die Forderung des Tages,* 1930)—all reaffirming the subtlety of Mann's perception and testifying to the alertness of his response to the cultural challenges of the time. Mann's intellectual convictions are based upon Nietzsche and the German conservative tradition, and spring at the same time from a lively sense of historical continuity and spiritual order. Apart from frequent tributes to those writers to whom he has felt himself most closely related (Novalis, Heine, Whitman, Fontane, Ibsen, Tolstoy, Conrad, Gide, and others), he has devoted one volume of studies, *Leiden und Grösse der Meister* (1935), to Goethe, Wagner, Platen, and Storm.

In a delightful story, *Unordnung und frühes Leid* (1926), he portrays, against the background of his own family and with melancholy irony, the moral and social confusion which resulted from the chaotic years of the European inflation of values. No less penetrating is the charming *Mario und der Zauberer* (1930), a "tragedy of travel" with "moral and political implications."

In the meantime, the plan was being formulated for what will certainly prove to be Mann's most profound and elaborate statement of his vision of man's timeless nature—though not, perhaps, his most pleasing work. A portfolio of illustrations depicting the story of Joseph, for which he was asked to write an introduction, suggested to him the subject of the novel, *Joseph und seine Brüder,* the first volume of which was not published until 1933. Not unlike *Der Zauberberg,* this impressive tale emphasizes the cultural obligations which a purposeful life imposes upon the human being. The depths of time, which had so fascinated Hans Castorp, and the barely tangible recesses of the human soul are now represented in terms of the perennial and typical man. "I thought it might be amusing to attempt, by means of a mythical psychology, a psychology of the myth." The biblical world is seen through the ever-sharpening eyes of the young Joseph, another Hans Castorp, whose environment, manners, and language are reproduced with meticulous archaeological accuracy, but who is, at the same time, himself endowed with the knowing perception of a modern observer. The four bulky volumes, *Die Geschichten Jaakobs* (1933), *Der junge Joseph* (1934), *Joseph in Aegypten* (1936), and *Joseph der Ernährer* (1944), represent Mann's most positive treatment of the social order outside of which civilized living is impossible. The broader problem of cultural unity has thus absorbed in Mann's later work the issue of the artist's personal relationship to society. Even in *Lotte in Weimar* (1939), which gives an account of the historic visit in 1816 of Werther's Lotte to the aged Goethe, the stress is not so much upon the problematical figure of the artist as upon the humanistic achievement of a man whose self-denying and stylized life is, to the bourgeois observer, not without strangeness and tragedy. In this book and in the short novel, *Die vertauschten Köpfe* (1940), the degree of Mann's detachment has at times become disturbing. Now and again, most distressingly in the *Joseph* novels, he tends to allow his pedagogical and discursive inclination to expand the form of the novel to such an extent that it appears to become merely a "series of essays in disguise." His talents as storyteller are unrivaled, but his style is often pedantic, pontifical, and mannered, and it is not seldom that he executes brilliant flourishes upon a surface of indifferent interest.

The scope and texture of Mann's work have steadily grown; the many memorable figures of his distinguished world, the Tonio Krögers and Buddenbrooks, the Aschenbachs and Hans Castorps, even the mythological characters of a re-created past, have appeared before us as ever more urgent reminders of the novelist's concern with the human chance of spiritual self-justification. If, in the earliest tales, it was the socially suspect artist who failed to assert himself against an uncomprehending bourgeoisie, the problem of man's adjustment to society and his mastery of the irrational by the power of his intelligence has of late become Mann's dominant theme. With his work the German novel has undoubtedly attained European rank, but in spite, or because, of the accuracy of his observation, he has, to some extent, remained the characteristic representative of an atomistic age. When, in the twenties, the mood of the time became revolutionary, it seemed to many that his voice and his preceptorial humanism had lost some of their persuasive force. Since his arrival in the United States, he has, once again, taken an active part in the discussion of current political issues (*The Coming Victory of Democracy*, 1938, *This Peace*, 1938, and other works), but where his defense of the democratic faith is more than a rhetorical gesture, it often rests upon reactionary premises; he has not achieved in the New World the effectiveness of argument or speech for which his earlier German essays had made him so distinguished. Yet he remains the outstanding representative of a great narrative tradition. Many other less brittle novelists may, in their work, have reflected the changing tide of contemporary feeling more directly and perhaps with more absorbing passion, but in intelligence, moral seriousness, and craftsmanship Thomas Mann has rarely been surpassed.

The concern of the German writer for the character and function of the spiritual life at the turn of the century was, of course, but one aspect of the general European reassessment of values. In France, Russia, and Scandinavia many serious voices had spoken, in hope or fear, of the imminent disintegration of the accepted order. But in Germany these voices were more radical than elsewhere; they were, in Nietzsche's sense, "nihilistic," and proclaimed a spiritual civil war, a revolution of the dissident bourgeoisie against its own members. They were not merely the expression of temporary social grievances and were only rarely motivated by proletarian convictions. Coming from the ranks of the middle class itself, they sought not primarily the establishment of a "progressive" society, but (like most German revolutionary movements) the rediscovery, the "restoration" of fundamental human resources. Nietzsche's pessimistic view of civilization, his excoriation of current bourgeois values, and his insistence upon what he called biological rather than idealistic standards seemed to carry the weight of plausible and ominous prophecy. As the superficial prosperity and ebullience of the new German state increased, the power of cultural criticism gained momentum and eventually developed into what must be called an apocalyptic sense of crisis without which neither the generation before nor that after the First World War can be fully understood.

Among the novelists there were few who did not protest against the sham pattern of the age. Gerhart Hauptmann's *Der Narr in Christo Emanuel Quint* (1910) and Hermann Burte's *Wiltfeber* (1912) show the mood of apprehension, but the acid work of the dramatist Frank Wedekind (1864–1918) is perhaps the clearest indication of the cynical despair and scepticism with which all contemporary values were being regarded. In spite of his obvious formal shortcomings Wedekind created the boldest and the most fascinating world of demoniacally dislocated bourgeois characters. His impulse is at all times antinaturalistic, and although his main theme is the horror of the brutality of sex, the manner of his prose dramas is romantic in the modern and ironic understanding of that word. At the same time, Wedekind's antierotic obsession is linked with an effective sense of the grotesque disequilibrium of middle-class society. Himself outside this world, he directs the brilliant beam of his implacable searchlight slantwise at the marginal accidents of the vast human circus. Between his dream-clear and unforgettable figures there exists no genuine communication; they are related to one another not by the conventional means of dramatic context, but by their precise and speechless function within a breathtaking histrionic act. The startling elements of his minstrelsy and the shrillness of his moralizing message reappear later in the sophisticated ballads of Paul Zech (b. 1881), Klabund (1891–1928), and Bertolt Brecht (b. 1898), in the "epic" theater of the late twenties, and, in a different medium, in the stark social caricatures of George Grosz.

But in Wedekind's successors the political impulse is much more succinct and even explicit to the point of being doctrinaire. The case of Heinrich Mann (b. 1871) is of particular interest. It may be that, in the long run, his pithy and brusque prose will wear better than his brother's cautious delicacy. In many respects Thomas Mann has remained the circumspect representative of a predominantly clinical age; Heinrich, on the other hand, has not merely surveyed and reflected, but time and again has challenged and struck out against the spirit of bourgeois servility and deceit in all its most repellent forms. Long before the actual collapse of imperial Germany, he recognized and denounced its fatal weaknesses. In his work that political indecision which characterized the early nineteenth-century novelists in Germany is significantly overcome. The targets of his attacks are varied, but they are always the telling symbols of human and political ineptness. In his first novel, *Im Schlaraffenland* (1900), he exposes the evil power of money and corrupt journalism; later (in *Professor Unrat*, 1905, *Die Armen*,

1917, and *Der Untertan,* written in 1914, published in 1918), he turns to individual and collective forms of the life which he held up to such drastic contempt. It is seldom that he chooses so delightful and limpid a theme as that of *Die kleine Stadt* (1909), where he evokes all the magic and melody of a small Italian community. In 1925 he focused once more upon the shattered image of the Wilhelmian age (*Der Kopf*) and in a number of recent studies, some of great historical sweep and vigor (e.g., *Die Jugend des Königs Henri Quatre,* 1935, *Die Vollendung des Königs Henri Quatre,* 1938), he presses home the advantages of one who never failed to warn against the imminent disaster which finally overtook Europe. If he was at one time denounced as a mere *Zivilisationsliterat,* preoccupied with what seemed ephemeral issues of political behavior, he has recently at least had the satisfaction of seeing his brother belatedly assume the very role of an eloquent political essayist which he himself had never hesitated to assign to the man of letters. The roots of Thomas's thinking are in the great tradition of German conservatism; Heinrich's lie in the emancipated liberalism of the French, in the penetrating precision of Stendhal, and in the savage honesty of Balzac and Maupassant. His intelligence is never merely ironical or frail, but uncompromisingly aggressive, and his most memorable human portraits, even in so diffuse a novel as *Die Göttinnen* (1902–1903), have much of the nightmarish and grotesque superreality of Dickens, Daumier, or Wedekind.

In the years between the appearance of Raabe's *Horacker* (1876) and Heinrich Mann's *Der Untertan* (1918), the form of cultural criticism had hardened, and its intention had gained in bitterness. But the sense of instability and crisis was not confined to the social and political discussion of the time. In all the imaginative arts throughout Europe the period before the First World War is characterized by an antirationalistic, indeed, a religious, groping for essential and spiritual values beyond the artificial confines of the bourgeois conventions of experience. The lively interest in Strindberg and Kierkegaard, in Baudelaire and the French symbolist poets, and the ever more fashionable preoccupation with Eastern, especially Russian literature, are sufficiently telling signs.

The minor fiction of Jakob Wassermann (1873–1934) represents in its subject matter the most persuasive and the most facile statement of the prevailing sense of the individual's merging into humanity or, it would be better to say, of man's individual responsibility for the whole of mankind. His novels, often flamboyant and mannered in form, are at once speculative and artificial in their problems. The properties of Balzac and Dostoevsky seem here superficially combined with a large measure of humanitarian feeling and a thoroughgoing analytical skill. But in spite of his technical insight (see *Die Kunst der Erzählung,* 1904) and his occasional brilliant successes as narrator, he has not achieved a single novel of major importance. Throughout his extensive work he has praised the redeeming power of humility, devotion, and surrender: not only in the two most spectacular of his novels, *Christian Wahnschaffe* (1919) and *Der Fall Maurizius* (1928), but still more plausibly in his earlier account of the strange foundling, *Caspar Hauser* (1908), does the rare individual, sensitive and nearly defeated by the common "indolence of the heart," emerge the greater for his suffering. Yet as his characters are charged, even overcharged, with pseudoreligious powers of compassion, so the external elements of his falsely realistic contemporary world become exorbitant and sensational. On the surface Wassermann's novels appear to be documents of present-day conflicts; but his social thinking was essentially sentimental and private. If it had been otherwise, Wassermann might now be regarded as the most expert craftsman of the naturalistic succession.

In their form these and other popular novels avoid the radical idiom which was to become so characteristic of the subsequent generation. Impressionist delicacy and naturalistic determinism had become equally suspect during the years before 1914. George's *Blätter für die Kunst* had prepared the attack upon both attitudes. The artist now demanded images which were not accidental but essential and absolutely valid; he insisted not so much upon an adherence to formal principles of external accuracy as upon an imaginative re-creation, an "ex-pression," of the commonly concealed core of any given thing or experience. Not the artist's impression of a stable world, but the intensity of his intuitive emotional grasp was now to be the source of his work. The reality which he was to represent was not to be a mere copy, a literal transcription of casual living, but a vision different from it in shape and more intensely spiritual in quality.

'TIS all in peeces, all cohaerence gone;
All just supply, and all Relation:
Prince, Subject, Father, Sonne, are things forgot,
For every man alone thinkes he hath got
To be a Phœnix, and that then can bee
None of that kinde, of which he is, but hee.

DONNE

IV

COHERENCE GONE

THE years between 1914 and 1944 must, in Germany, be understood as the successive stages of a thirty years' revolution in which each decade develops its own pattern of outward action and spiritual coherence. The outbreak of the First World War brought to a spectacular climax the long-foreseen collapse of nineteenth-century values; the political disintegration, which was at its severest in 1918, radically and cruelly affected the entire life of the German people in the years of the subsequent economic inflation. Later, between 1925 and 1934, the inner resources of the nation were once again being mobilized, and in one form or another, liberal or conservative, the threatened human resolve began to re-emerge. The Nazi era, with its extreme and desperate forms of physical and intellectual ruthlessness, finally forced the revolutionary crisis in values to an apocalyptic climax.

The manifold lines of the cultural life during this period are not easy to retrace. As we approach the present, it cannot be surprising if representative figures belonging to different generations, and divergent attitudes and idioms, find themselves side by side in uneasy company. They are, however, from the very beginning held together by two powerful brackets of experience: the one a persistent and all-pervading sense of crisis, and the other the attempt to recover or establish forms of belief and behavior.

Throughout this revolutionary era, the figure of Nietzsche determines all efforts at analysis or synthesis. Even the youth movement, whatever its immediate objective, would not have become so generous and effective a ferment if it had not received its direction from the radicalism of Nietzsche's challenges. These self-conscious group organizations and ideologically ever more militant *Bünde* (such as the *Wandervogel*, 1896, and *Pfadfinder*, 1911), in which the young bourgeois rebelled against the old, were to exercise a highly formative influence upon the first revolutionary decade. Their emotional and anti-intellectual attitude brought the coming generation to a determined state of spiritual or, more frequently, pseudospiritual mobilization. In every phase of the subsequent literature, the feeling among the young, either of radical disillusionment or of revolutionary emancipation, remains one of the prominent pathological themes.

But Nietzsche's images proved most stirring where they stimulated a re-examination of the historical foundations of the time. The interest in the philosophical margin of history had, of course, for long been peculiarly lively among the German writers. At this point, in 1918, Spengler's *Untergang des Abendlandes* supplied a cultural interpretation of the broadest sweep. Written by a mathematician with the most incisive elegance of thought and style, it suggested a new and fascinating type of morphological speculation. Its aim was not so much a genuine historical analysis as, rather, an attempt, with the tools and stencils of the natural sciences, to superimpose a spiritual frame upon the complex reality of history. It was a belated materialistic document, and, together with the more indefinite reflections of Count Hermann Keyserling's *Reisetagebuch eines Philosophen* (1919), it represented an intellectual pseudosynthesis, the effect of which was altogether negative.

Even in the arts, in music and painting, the disintegration or, it would be better to say, the deliberate reorganization of the pattern of things seen and felt became plainly apparent. In the early works of Munch, Gauguin, Van Gogh, Picasso, and Kokoschka, in Schönberg's *Pierrot lunaire* (1912), in the statues of Lehmbruck (1881–1919) and Ernst Barlach (1870–1938, "Vision," 1912), the characteristic use of purposeful distortion suggested the striking range of the new sensibility. In all these artists, most movingly, perhaps, in the work of the painter Franz Marc (1880–1916), ecstatic intensity of feeling has shattered conventional forms, and a new, inner organ of perception seems to be at work. The expressionist manner was, of course, not confined to German literature; but in the hectic decade after the First World War it had its most enthusiastic supporters in Germany. As early as 1910 some of its tenets were expounded in two periodicals with the pointed titles, *Sturm* (edited by H. Walden) and *Aktion* (edited by F. Pfemfert), followed in 1913 by R. Schickele's *Die weissen Blätter*. Hermann Bahr (1863–1934), the mercurial Viennese who had, in 1891, proclaimed the end of naturalism (*Die Überwindung des Naturalismus*), now outlined in his brief and popular pamphlet (*Expressionismus*, 1916) the main features of expressionism. A vast literature of enthusiastic and pseudocritical adherence to the new creed paraphrased the anti-bourgeois, pacifist, and revolutionary (activist) nature of the new theses.

But only in the work of the lyrical poets did the expressionistic doctrine release poetic energies that were to become a living part of the literary substance. Kurt Pinthus' comprehensive and crystallizing anthology, *Menschheitsdämmerung* (1920), and Rudolf Kayser's *Verkündigung* (1921) reveal the variety of the expressionist themes and temperaments. The early poets, Georg Heym (1887–1912), Georg Trakl (1887–1914), Ernst Stadler (1883–1914), and August Stramm (1874–1915), prophetically anticipate the terrifying shadows of the war years. In the poems of Gerrit Engelke (1892–1918), Heinrich Lersch

(1889–1936), Max Barthel (b. 1893), Karl Bröger (b. 1886), and Johannes Robert Becher (b. 1891), the fervor of inspiration and rebellion against the demons of a mechanized age illuminates their proletarian and humanitarian motives. The younger generation, emphatic in their denunciation of war (see Franz Diederich's pacifist anthology, *Von unten auf,* 1911), nevertheless reflect the political preoccupation of the time.

The private experience predominates in the baroque achievements of only a few of the expressionist poets —in Theodor Däubler (1876–1934, *Das Nordlicht,* 1910), in Else Lasker-Schüler (b. 1876, *Styx,* 1902, and *Hebräische Balladen,* 1913), and chiefly in Ernst Barlach, who remains, among these, the most memorable. His work (*Der tote Tag,* 1912, *Der arme Vetter,* 1918, and *Der blaue Boll,* 1926) is ostensibly dramatic, but it is actually sustained by the intense metaphysical lyricism of a poet in whom the powerful visions of a northern German temperament are blended with the deep religious mysticism of the great Russian novelists. Even the earlier poetry of Franz Werfel (b. 1890, *Der Weltfreund,* 1912, *Wir sind,* 1913, *Einander,* 1915, and *Gedichte,* 1927) revolves around the emotional experience of a human being who strives to push beyond the radical isolation of the individual. Not only in its religious seriousness, but by its brilliant musical cadences, it is reminiscent of the younger Rilke. In spite of Werfel's antiwar sentiments, which he shares with his revolutionary contemporaries, his poetry has few of the strident artificialities of the expressionist fraternity. Only now and then does it break into the rebellious cry of the later drama.

For it was in the expressionistic drama that the conventions of feeling and form were most strikingly and most consistently denied. Here, in the lyrical and monodramatic plays of Reinhard Sorge (1892–1916, *Der Bettler,* 1912), Walter Hasenclever (1890–1941, *Der Sohn,* 1914), Fritz von Unruh (b. 1885), Ernst Toller (1893–1939), and Franz Werfel, or in the sharp and bizarre social indictments of Carl Sternheim (1878–1943), Georg Kaiser (1878–1945, *Von Morgens bis Mitternacht,* 1916), and Arnolt Bronnen (b. 1895), the shiftless and fearful undercurrents of life were cast into startling images and intellectualized symbols, and represented in generalized actions and characters which were stripped of their superficial plausibility.

Especially in the father-son motif, which is common to the poets and dramatists of the time, the issues between the generations are now pointedly and defiantly stated. The problem was, of course, not new: in some of the earlier novels of Emil Strauss (b. 1866, *Freund Hein,* 1902), Friedrich Huch (1873–1913, *Peter Michel,* 1901), Hermann Hesse (b. 1877, *Unterm Rad,* 1906), and Otto Stoessl (b. 1875, *Morgenroth,* 1912) it had been treated with the melancholy of great poetic refinement; but in its present exaggerated form it is a symbolic indication of the sharp tension between the absolute demands of the young and the relativistic opportunism of the past.

At the same time the typically flamboyant "cry" uttered in an unresponsive "space" required new patterns of presentation; the expressionistic theater of men like Jessner, Martin, Fehling, or Piscator, conveyed the intention within a grotesquely dissolved architectural frame and through the distorted but intense and rhythmical tones and gestures of depersonalized actors. It provided an adequate, if puzzling, medium for a revolutionary and uprooted generation. In the manner of the eighteenth century, but now directed towards the emerging concepts of an aggressively proletarian society, it emphasized its moral obligation. Few of the expressionistic plays have survived the psychological climate in which they were conceived. They remain essentially the telling documents of a period of frenzied vertigo, but they testify no less to an idealistic resurgence in which the collective experience of political and social instability and defeat found its compensating poetic forms in hyperbolic effusion and frantic commotion.

The same measure of formal dissolution was not, perhaps, feasible in the realm of expressionistic prose fiction. But the German novelist of that time shares with his contemporaries in France and England a will to redefine in theory and practice the shape and function of narrative art. The early works of Kasimir Edschmid

(b. 1890), his programmatical treatise on poetic expressionism, *Über den Expressionismus in der Literatur* (1919), and his collection of short stories, *Die sechs Mündungen* (1915), show this intention unmistakably. In the novels of Alfred Döblin (b. 1878), Franz Werfel, Erwin Guido Kolbenheyer (b. 1878), Leonhard Frank (b. 1882), and Hermann Stehr (1864–1940), the spirit of social and private rebellion and the quest for a new faith are pressed into an explosive and belligerent narrative idiom. In these writings the real purpose of the expressionist attitude becomes clear: it is a radical attempt to maintain the force and validity of metaphysical aspirations in a fundamentally antispiritual world, the debilitated forms of which require re-examination.

The work of Alfred Döblin, at all times significantly concerned with the particular formal possibilities of a given intellectual situation, is of some distinction. Beginning with speculative stories and philosophical essays, he turns during the war to a complex kind of fiction which is, in spite of certain exorbitant and fantastic elements, sharply realistic and obviously true to Döblin's diagnostic disposition. *Die drei Sprünge des Wang-Lun* (1915)—the story of a Chinese rebel who is moved by a strong religious impulse—was followed by a picturesquely fictional study of *Wallenstein* (1920). In 1929 appeared Döblin's most generally known novel, *Berlin Alexanderplatz,* in which the steadiness of his eye, the analytical quality of the trained psychiatrist, and a remarkable precision of speech combine to produce not only a sociologically relevant picture, but a moving account of the inhumanity of the city. Although it was at the time hailed as the characteristic example of a "new objectivity," it is, in fact, the work of a decidedly naturalistic perception. Döblin joined other refugees abroad, and among the politically minded writers continued to be one of the most clear-headed. Not only such works as *Babylonische Wanderungen* (1934) or the South American impressions in *Das Land ohne Tod* (1937–1938), but the brief and suggestive pamphlet upon German literature in exile (*Die deutsche Literatur im Ausland seit 1933*, 1938), "a dialogue between politics and art," testify to his intelligence and his integrity.

The memory of Nietzsche's intellectual criticism and Freud's insistence upon the symbolic nature of all explicit acts is, during the first revolutionary decade, apparent in every kind of prose writing. Nowhere are these elements more significantly rendered than in the neoromantic and surrealist novels of Franz Kafka (1883–1924), whose influence upon our generation, particularly in England and America, has been remarkable and profound.

Kafka was born in Prague of a well-to-do middle-class family, in an atmosphere dominated by his father's personality (see the "Brief an den Vater," 1919) and reminiscent of the earlier years of Proust.

Devotion to literature was his real concern and it was only the slowness and conscientiousness of his writing that seemed to make it difficult for him to gain a livelihood by it. Little of his work was published during his lifetime; indeed, none of his three novels, *Der Prozess* (1925), *Das Schloss* (1926), and *Amerika* (1927), were completed. Most of his reputation rests upon the posthumous publication (happily undertaken by his friend, Max Brod, against Kafka's own wishes) of an impressive number of short stories, parables, aphorisms, journals, and letters in the *Gesammelte Schriften* (1935–1937).

In his first published work, a collection of prose, *Betrachtung* (1913), and two short stories, "Der Heizer" (1913—later the first chapter of his novel *Amerika*) and "Das Urteil" (1913), he established the main theme of his work, which he soon elaborated in the "ecstatically conceived" story, *Die Verwandlung* (1916). In 1918, during months of serious illness in the country, he began the first chapter of his novel, *Das Schloss*. A few delicate short stories published under the title *Ein Landarzt*, were followed in 1919 by the significant tale, *In der Strafkolonie*, and one year before his death he completed a last volume of characteristically lucid and mobile prose, *Ein Hungerkünstler*.

The three major novels, *Amerika, Der Prozess,* and *Das Schloss,* form, in the words of the editor, Max Brod, "a trilogy of loneliness." Like every other work of Kafka's, they reflect, in a seriously religious sense, the experience of human isolation and the pathos of exclusion. Man, forever aware of "guilt," is compelled to face the "trial" of life in a universe whose pattern and coherence are fundamentally uncertain and incomprehensible. The God of Kafka's world is as terrible and fascinating as Jehovah, and however fervently the poet's Job-like characters may wrestle with "the law," there is for them no ultimate consolation. They are but troubled marionettes who can find no escape from the realization of overwhelming frustration. Man's life passes in a series of crises in which the veiled presence of "the law," acting through impersonal agencies (the government, the police, the office, the castle, and so forth), demonstrates the futility of human effort. Much of Kafka's imaginative thinking is drawn from Jewish folk literature and the Talmud; but the tenets of his belief should be related to Pascal, the existential philosophy of Kierkegaard, and the contemporary theology of crisis (Karl Barth). In its radically eschatological nature his symbolic faith is reminiscent of Dostoevsky and Strindberg. The use of minutely detailed, irrational, dream landscapes in which strangely associated phenomena seem suspended in an unintelligible void indicates Kafka's nearness to the expressionist and surrealist writers. Religious and social conflicts meet at this point, for the plausibility and realism of his *petit-bourgeois* world is deceptive; his human beings find themselves curiously out of touch with their own setting, and are unable to foresee their own chances of survival or destruction. At the same time Kafka is not without an active sense of defiance: even the laconic humor of some of his tales rests upon a powerful faith in what Kafka himself calls the "indestructible"; in those grotesque scenes of moral suspense in which the pathetic creature finds himself caught in the grip of an inescapable mechanism, he reminds us not only of Charlie Chaplin and Walt Disney but of Poe and Dickens.

In spite of the subtlety and precision of his prose style, Kafka is not, compared to his contemporaries, Proust, Joyce, or Thomas Mann, one of the accomplished novelists. He is rather, with Rilke, the supremely religious writer of an age in which man, caught in inevitable perplexity and doubt, seems incapable of personal salvation.

Near Kafka and Rilke stands Franz Werfel (b. 1890), who, though a decidedly lesser figure, is the third representative of a specifically eastern form of religious seriousness. Born like them in Prague, he began his career with a series of reflective poems in which he attempted to transcend the modern sense of spiritual isolation and intellectual arrogance. Throughout his work he has remained true to this theme and has continued to speak as the eloquent representative of inward idealism. In a significant essay, *Realismus und Innerlichkeit* (1931), he has pointed to the creative poles of his art. A number of spectacular and, at times, baffling expressionistic dramas (e.g., *Spiegelmensch,* 1920, and *Bocksgesang,* 1921) were followed in 1924 by a historical tragedy, *Juarez und Maximilian,* and in 1926 by *Paulus unter den Juden*—his first attempt to sustain the efficacy of the individual by a fervent and, above all, active belief in a spiritual deity. In 1924 also appeared his *Verdi,* a fanciful but moving account of the tragedy of the aging artist, written in a swift and conscientious prose rarely again attained in his more recent work. Two short novels, *Der Tod des Kleinbürgers* (1927) and *Der Abituriententag* (1928), show Werfel's gifts most attractively: in the one he gives an unforgettable portrait of an Austrian *petit-bourgeois,* in the other a penetrating analysis of a complicated psychological relationship. Unlike Döblin, Werfel has never been explicitly interested in social or political issues as such; they are, rather, problematical aspects of his central concern with the sources and modes of human salvation. In his latest novels, from *Barbara* (1929) to *Die vierzig Tage des Musa Dagh* (1933) and the appealing *Das Lied von Bernadette* (1941), he has reached, in spite of a somewhat ponderous manner, a certain measure of spiritual maturity. What appeared in the hectic productions of the twenties as a subtle but indistinct groping for emotional self-justification has now become the simple and humble recognition of human dependence upon the life-giving and unfailing presence of a creative God.

MEMORY is an aspect of the present. Indeed, on a level of ultimate comprehension, all memory will seem a form of poetic anticipation.

NOVALIS

V

RECOLLECTION AND RECOVERY

BY 1924, the year of Kafka's death and the year in which Thomas Mann's *Zauberberg* sums up the conflicting tendencies of a bewildering age, the first revolutionary decade, and with it the expressionistic interlude, had come to an end. It is true that for a short time the radical theses of social revolution continued to be advanced in the shrill and dissonant manner of the political theater (Bertolt Brecht, b. 1898, Ferdinand Bruckner, b. 1891, Friedrich Wolf, b. 1888). But the dramatist's voice had lost the dithyrambic note of private agony. If a new social and intellectual order had not yet been found, if a common denominator of accepted beliefs had not been established, there nevertheless began to emerge from among the poets and artists signs of a recovery of the emotional equilibrium. The terms "matter-of-factness" (*Neue Sachlichkeit*) and "magic realism" offered themselves conveniently for the critical discussion of the change in perspective. Actually, the firmer and less sentimental frame in which life now seemed to gain coherence, and which gave a certain stability of vision to the poets, owed its preliminary strength to more than one element. It was not, at any rate, a casual reflection of temporary economic conditions, but rather, in the work of the significant writers, a decision to survey with utmost soberness the moral resources from which the contemporary life was to derive its validity.

This combination of sobriety and resoluteness must be emphasized; for in it lies the significance of this decade, which would otherwise count as a mere phase in the long process of disillusionment through which German literature, even during its most extravagant years, had been moving. Cultural criticism, as we have seen, was one of the significant impulses of the preceding two generations. But at this point the measure of disintegration was so overwhelming, the meaning of the state—indeed, the very premises of all human assumptions—were so completely reduced that only the self-denying restraint of clinical detachment (cf. the early work of Gottfried Benn, b. 1886, *Fleisch,* 1917, *Morgue,* 1923) seemed to lead to a promising diagnosis. Quite properly, the term, *Neue Sachlichkeit,* was first applied (by the art critic, Gustav Hartlaub) to the evidence of visible forms as the painters (e.g., Otto Dix) and architects presented it. Both the work of Le Corbusier and the courageous *avant-garde* group of the Bauhaus moved, with a radicalism puzzling to the bourgeois, towards forms of building which would correspond to contemporary patterns of living. The extreme frugality of the designs of Walter Gropius and Kurt May suggested a wholly unsentimental concentration upon the most direct measure of practical planning and the immediate function of materials. The word *Gebrauch* ("usable") became an attribute of specific praise, and it was not only among the painters and musicians but among the writers that the new idiom was soon and vigorously recognized. The word *reportage,* in its restrained meaning of an eyewitness account, indicated the utmost measure of precision.

That so exacting a notion of impersonality did not soon meet the fate of all naturalistic impulses was due to the fact that the new techniques were practiced by men who were not disillusioned but rather sceptical in the extreme. The two terms are not, of course, identical. To be sceptical of the pretenses by which a world in transition hopes to sustain its traditional social practices is not the same as to be indifferent to them. Indeed, just as in the case of Soviet realism, the German *Sachlichkeit* is inevitably coupled with a direct and radical political insight. The quiet and reserved reporting of Heinrich Hauser (b. 1901) and the forceful social criticism in the novels of B. Traven are not, perhaps, as telling as the uncompromising bareness in the work of Bertolt Brecht, probably the most aggressive and consequential of all the younger communist poets. In opposition to the accepted understanding of dramatic structure, he has developed a type of "epic theater" which is, in effect, an attempt to produce in the spectator, not so much the moral catharsis of the Aristotelian drama as an attitude of immediate and direct political judgment. The didactic object of Brecht's dramatic experiments is at times concealed by his unconventional approach to the problems of staging. With the help of every possible technical device—the projection of documents, scenes from contemporary films, and musical support—he elaborates and underlines the implications of the thesis presented by the dramatist. Brecht's *Dreigroschenoper* became, partly through Kurt Weill's suggestive music but also because of its terse mixture of social scepticism and sentimental irony, the most symptomatic theatrical event of the late twenties. Even more characteristic of his political intentions are his *Versuche* (1930–1932) in one of which (*Der Flug der Lindberghs*) the bleakness of statement is supported by Paul Hindemith's astringent musical score.

Even Brecht's severe theatrical enterprise would not have been effective if it had not been for obliquely and ironically introduced moments of stark sentimentality. It is, indeed, this mixture of detachment and melodramatic pathos which made the work of these pseudo-objective writers so widely popular. This is as true of Erich Kästner's (b. 1899) poetry as it is of the entertaining pastiche of vitality and exaggerated slapstick in the plays of Carl Zuckmayer (b. 1896, *Der fröhliche Weinberg*, 1925, and *Schinderhannes*, 1927).

The younger generation, generally dislocated by the aftermath of the First World War, now surveys the shattered frame of its life in a spirit of detached sobriety but, nevertheless, driven by a desire to discover and establish promising forms of political action. Oskar Maria Graf's (b. 1894) *Wir sind Gefangene* (1927) is one of the strongest accounts of the physical and moral impact of the war and postwar years upon those born shortly before 1900; Ernst Glaeser's (b. 1902) *Jahrgang 1902* (1928) relates most succinctly the disillusionment of the men to whom neither past nor future offers steadying prospects. Other works in the same self-critical tone (Peter Martin Lampel's [b. 1894] play, *Revolte im Erziehungshaus*, 1929, and Hans Fallada's [b. 1893] successful novel *Kleiner Mann, was nun?* 1932) emphasize from the desperate vantage point of the young some of the origins of the social and political disorder. Such powerful and demonic books as B. Traven's *Totenschiff* (1926) or his *Die Brücke im Dschungel* (1929), even though they do not confine themselves to the German scene, see deeper into the roots of the coming conflict. They are among the most stirring of the social narratives of the time, and point with their grim and visionary realism beyond Kafka towards the manner of some of the younger refugee writers, such as Anna Seghers (b. 1900, *Aufstand der Fischer von St. Barbara*, 1928, and *Das siebte Kreuz*, 1942) and the Hungarian, Arthur Koestler (b. 1905), who have developed a striking balance between aggressive antifascist criticism and a surrealist sense of compelling irrational forces.

In Hermann Hesse's *Der Steppenwolf* (1927), in Hermann Broch's (b. 1886) broad trilogy, *Die Schlafwandler* (1931–1932), or in Robert Musil's (1880–1943) ironically brittle *Der Mann ohne Eigenschaften* (1930), the moral deflation of the age finds its most telling expression: all bourgeois forms of life are here glaringly exposed and seem permanently broken; there remains only the challenging reality of man's preoccupation with the plain business of living.

Hermann Hesse's career as poet and novelist reaches into the first decade of the century and is divided into two distinct and equally remarkable phases: during the first he created from his Swabian background a series of subdued and musical novels of private, provincial, and melancholy lyricism (*Peter Camenzind*, 1904, *Unterm Rad*, 1906, *Gertrud*, 1910, and *Demian*, 1919). The war then forced his thinking into a new direction; from its spiritual wreckage he hoped at least to rescue the fragments of moral and humane strength; Nietzsche's scathing cultural visions (*Zarathustras Wiederkehr*, 1920) and the experience of Eastern mysticism (*Aus Indien*, 1913, and *Siddharta*, 1922) became to him positive sources of regeneration. If in his earlier novels he had turned from the rich and colorful world with the self-conscious gesture of the overwhelmed and weary, he advanced now beyond the expressionistic fervor of personal suffering towards a more sober acceptance of the new and deeply transformed human situation. *Der Steppenwolf,* although by no means his most attractive book, is a revealing and startling portrait, not only of the individual, Harry Haller, but of a generation whose two warring souls, one wild and lawless, the other bourgeois and confined, can find no rest in a shattered age. Hesse's solution is reinforced by his religious humanism: man, who has to this Franciscan poet (see *Franz von Assisi,* 1904) always seemed frail and insufficient, must take the terror of the world upon himself, and in self-denying love and devotion create within the incoherent chaos of the time a small area of meaningful living. This, at least, is the tentative theme of Hesse's last two novels, *Narziss und Goldmund* (1930) and the serene and resolute *Glasperlenspiel* (1943). With these two narratives, especially the latter, in which he recalls the ideals of hierarchical service and devotion set forth in Goethe's "pedagogical province," he closes a wide and solemn circle of inquiry, and returns in temper and melody, but upon a higher plane of creative renunciation, to the calm Alemannic character of his first writings.

Broch's work springs from altogether different intellectual premises; it is a striking example of a new type of European cultural portraiture in which scientific speculation and poetic imagination are combined to reproduce all the incoherent variety of contemporary experience. In what Broch calls the *polyhistoric* form of the novel, he blends many creative devices, and at least in this bold attempt to find an adequate medium for the complexity of rational and irrational impulses, he belongs in the distinguished company of Joyce and Gide. In the first volume of the *Schlafwandler* trilogy (*Pasenow oder die Romantik*) the stagnation and disintegration of the spiritual life is revealed beneath the thin ice of a deceptive romantic ideology. The central figure of the second volume (*Esch oder die Anarchie*) represents the drift from pseudobourgeois clerkdom to the despair of a godless and valueless life. *Huguenau oder die Sachlichkeit* finally leaves no doubt of the collapse of all organic coherence, and shows, in a more discursive fashion (as in the intercalated reflections upon "The Decay of Values"), the escape into surrogate forms of belief. This remarkable and complex triptych is Broch's central achievement. Several thoughtful minor publications (especially the novel, *Die unbekannte Grösse,* 1933) reiterate the existential elements in Broch's philosophical position. His latest work, *Der Tod des Vergil* (1945), one of the most remarkable contributions to German literature in exile, is an unusually stirring prose poem which interprets the visions of Virgil and that age from whose bloodshed and convulsions Christianity was soon to emerge.

It may be that the writers of the late twenties, with their instinctive desire for direct political action, had their eyes too closely upon the immediate present. Their only, or at least their most plausible, means of gaining creative distance from their own problematical experience was the ironical gesture. It was, perhaps, natural that under the overwhelming pressure of startling technological, social, and political events, certain historical resources which had influenced and even supported the thinking of the preceding generations should have lost much of their efficacy. Those were, after all, the years when America, the enviable "land without history," was rediscovered, and a strangely one-sided image of it was enthusiastically affirmed by the younger writers who wished to shake off the paralyzing shackles of ever-binding traditions and inherited obligations to the past.

But to be a poet in a traditionless age is an intolerable disadvantage; it is thus not surprising that, even among those who recognized the singular nature of the present crisis, an attempt was made to relate the baffling life of the decade to the evidence of recent memories, without escaping into a superficially more attractive and less burdensome past. It is at this point that the forces of recollection contribute tentatively towards a new firmness of purpose and a new sense of inner stability. For the value of all contemporary literature must be measured by the manner in and degree to which the writer can detect and mobilize the moral resources of the age. The recognition of this fact is, of course, not a German event alone; it is characteristic of all the major figures of the day. But what is significant for German literature is that the double theme of recollection and stability is being developed not in a mood of idyllic and quietistic sentimentality, but in terms of a resolute acceptance of the inevitable terror of life. Recent German literature, even though it seems at times to employ the setting and devices of escapist literature, is in its motives and beliefs essentially tragic. Wherever the German poet recognizes circumstances in which man is compelled, without prospect of success, to bring the utmost of his human strength and intelligence into operation, whether in society or nature, in the present or the past, he seizes upon a subject which seems to him supremely challenging and peculiarly congenial.

Such a recovery of human resolution is the cardinal theme of the third revolutionary decade. The early signs of it appear among some of the novelists of the late twenties who focus anew upon the memories of the First World War. The impact of those four cataclysmic years had, of course, been immense. To the expressionists they had conjured up eschatological visions of radical evil; now, in a mood of calm recollection, the poet seems more disposed to accept in them the moral challenge of a supremely precarious life. Remarque's popular *Im Westen nichts Neues* (1929) was one of the first but not one of the most substantial of the war books. It is, rather, in the moving pages of Hans Carossa's unheroic yet resolute *Rumänisches Tagebuch* (1924), in the volume of *Kriegsbriefe gefallener Studenten* (1928), in Ludwig Renn's documentary *Krieg* (1928), in Rudolf G. Binding's disciplined *Aus dem Kriege* (1925), in Sigmund Graff and Carl Hintze's popular play, *Die endlose Strasse* (1929), in Joachim von der Goltz's *Der Baum von Cléry* (1934), and in the sharply realistic and detached work of Joseph Magnus Wehner (b. 1891), Edwin Erich Dwinger (b. 1898), and especially Ernst Jünger (b. 1895) that there emerges a poetic sensibility which far transcends the obvious subject matter of the war and leads away from mere optimistic or pessimistic speculation directly into the stern idiom of what contemporary German critics sometimes broadly call *existential* issues. None of these writers is in any sense romantic; their works demonstrate, on the contrary, the enormously important discovery that the technological and social changes of the last century have not decreased the perennial threat with which irrational forces confront the unstable life of man, and that only the constant and total exercise of all human virtues, physical as well as moral and intellectual, will establish the vital harmony that can and must sustain a culture.

This sense of a perpetual and fearful elemental fascination is one of the most conspicuous qualities of Ernst Jünger's work. His experience as an officer in the First World War supplied the substance and material of his first book, *In Stahlgewittern* (1920), in which he struck the characteristic theme of extreme action coupled with precise intellectual insight and soldierly pathos. Several volumes, not mainly of a narrative but of an essentially observational and reflective nature, followed. An account of adventures in southern France and northern Africa, *Afrikanische Spiele* (1936), places him in the formal neighborhood of Emil Strauss; but his proper vehicle is not so much the novel as the contemplative essay (*Das abenteuerliche Herz, Figuren und Capriccios,* 1929, new ed., 1938, and *Blätter und Steine,* 1934), in which his "stereoscopic" perception is rendered through imagery of extraordinary "perspective" power.

The political implications of his attitude—which is, in some regards, reminiscent of T. E. Lawrence—have had considerable influence upon the present generation. On one occasion Jünger examined in detail the social and emotional structure of the contemporary worker (*Der Arbeiter,* 1932); but it is in the soldier and his reflective counterpart, the poet, that Jünger recognizes the human type in which the supreme qualities of alertness, discipline, intelligence, and sensitiveness appear most strikingly. Jünger is an individualist, and although much of his work is drawn from experiences of the wars (cf. *Der Kampf als inneres Erlebnis,* 1922, *Feuer und Blut,* 1925, and *Das Wäldchen 125,* 1925), he should not be accused of the kind of German militaristic thinking that is so justly suspected. Indeed, in two of his recent books, the mythological parable, *Auf den Marmor-Klippen* (1939), and the diary of his months in 1940 as an officer in France, *Gärten und Strassen* (1942), Jünger writes urgently (though not without occasionally resorting to an elliptical paraphrase) of the threat to deep-rooted cultural values by the forces of undisciplined inhumanity and barbarian dissolution. Yet, the vigor of Jünger's intelligence does not merely emerge in the bald terms of philosophical propositions. His thought is always conveyed with the precision of one to whom the distinction between the observable fact and the irrational perspective is only one of degree and intensity. Dream imagery is, therefore, one of his most frequent devices, and his vision of nature has, at times, the puzzling coherence of a surrealist landscape. By his devotion to the civilized and civilizing qualities of language (e.g., *Geheimnisse der Sprache*, 1939), he has produced, in a series of successively more significant works, some of the finest prose now being written in Germany; it is lithe, energetic, unsentimental, and radiant. If the term "magic realism" should be applied at all, Jünger's work would most properly deserve it.

The First World War, whether contemplated as an individual experience or as a powerful and all-absorbing collective effort, is only the most conspicuous among the many tentative motives of recollection and reorientation. The use of even broader and more remote historical settings is another aspect of the same trend. This preoccupation with the past is, as we have said, not a mere escape into a less precarious yesterday; it has, indeed, none of the sentimental and idyllic characteristics of the historical novel. For it projects, with that remarkable German fondness for metaphor, the issues and problems of the present into the most revealing phases of the past, and demonstrates, wherever its intention is positive, occasions of exemplary human virtue; where it is critical and accusatory, it is, in the main, concerned with the evidence during the past hundred years of the disintegration of the bourgeois order.

The ponderous volumes of Wilhelm Schäfer's *Dreizehn Bücher der deutschen Seele* (1922), Paul Ernst's *Kaiserbuch* (1923–1928), or Otto Gmelin's (1886–1940) *Das neue Reich* (1930) are indications of the one tendency; Bruno Brehm's (b. 1892) account of the decline of the Austro-Hungarian Empire (*Apis und Este*, 1931, *Das war das Ende*, 1932, and *Weder Kaiser noch König*, 1933) or Joseph Roth's *Radetzkymarsch* (1932) illustrate the other. But there are many novelists who present current problems in historical disguise, and it is not seldom that their popular effectiveness is increased by a strong admixture, not only of adventure, but of strident patriotism. In the work of Hans Grimm (b. 1875), for instance, extreme and exclusive political motives would serve as little more than a persistent and monotonous theme if it were not for a striking narrative gift which appears advantageously in his collections of short stories (*Südafrikanische Novellen,* 1913, *Der Gang durch den Sand,* 1916, and *Der Richter in der Karu,* 1930). In these tales Grimm develops a taciturn style which, with its stress upon the relationships of family and community, lies somewhere between the saga and the political dossier. His widely discussed and substantial novel, *Volk ohne Raum* (1926), is an irregular but concentrated account of adverse experiences in Southwest Africa. In spite of its unrelieved seriousness, the integrity of its observation and the poignancy of its human portraiture give it weight among the mass of semihistorical fiction in which the pride and tribulations of Germans abroad supply the all-absorbing subject matter. Josef Ponten's (1883–1941) *Volk auf dem Wege* (5 vols., 1930–1941) and the novels of German life outside the Reich (Adolf Meschendörfer, b. 1877, Hans Watzlik, b. 1879, Erwin Wittstock, b. 1899, Heinrich Zillich, b. 1898) belong to this group; they will be remembered chiefly as impressive documents of the tenacity of the national character.

Most of these works, especially such monoliths as Hans Friedrich Blunck's (b. 1888) *Urvätersaga* (1925–1928) or even the gothic and rebarbative novels of Erwin Guido Kolbenheyer are not easily appreciated without elaborate spiritual premises and will remain, at best, tempting hieroglyphs to the foreign reader.

Erwin Guido Kolbenheyer, born in 1878 in Budapest and educated in Karlsbad, is perhaps the most powerful representative of the contemporary German effort to treat metaphysical concerns in terms, not of "intellectual" spiritualism, but of biological and naturalistic insights. Like Paul Ernst he recognized, most explicitly in his major theoretical study, *Die Bauhütte* (1925), the collapse of all forms of rational idealism. Several discursive prose works reiterate this conviction: a volume of essays, *Stimme* (1930), is devoted to certain political considerations of a vigorously conservative nature; a profound discussion of the aesthetics of the German novel is contained in the pamphlet, *Wie wurde der deutsche Roman Dichtung?* (1937); and in a series of reflections upon Goethe (1937) he recognizes the "biological" nature of the poet's achievement. Neither as a dramatist (*Die Brücke,* 1929, *Heroische Leidenschaften,* 1929, *Gregor und Heinrich,* 1934) nor as a lyrical poet (*Lyrisches Brevier,* 1929) has he attained complete fusion of thought and feeling in imaginative creation; but it is in his novels (*Amor Dei,* 1908, *Meister Joachim Pausewang,* 1910, the *Paracelsus* trilogy, 1917, 1922, 1926, and *Das gottgelobte Herz,* 1938), all of them written in a purposely archaic language, that Kolbenheyer has accomplished a convincing form of historical narrative in which the *ingenium teutonicum* asserts itself as a cultural force of remarkable "plasmatic capacity."

Kolbenheyer's work lacks the transparent ease of such well-known writers of historical fiction as Alfred Neumann (b. 1895), Bruno Frank (1887–1945), or Stefan Zweig (1881–1942), whose books state not so much the weight of conservatively conceived perennial values as, rather, the contemporary and threatened pattern of liberal living. Stefan Zweig represented in his best years something of the civilized, if at times overrefined, psychological miniature craftsmanship for which Lytton Strachey had set a persuasive and masterly pattern in England. Zweig's many historical portraits are not without a certain brilliant incisiveness; he had a clear, if rarely profound, sense of character. In his shorter stories (*Erstes Erlebnis,* 1911, *Amok,* 1923, and *Verwirrung der Gefühle,* 1926) he combines an analytical temper with a brisk and overdeliberate, almost expressionistic, speech; occasionally (cf. *Drei Meister,* 1919, and *Erasmus,* 1935) a decided intellectual affinity to his subject enhances his effectiveness. On the whole, Zweig's reputation rests upon the minor literary virtues of versatility, intelligence, and a lively pen.

It is understandable that in such a situation, many serious Germans would like to say with Jakob Burckhardt: "There is nothing that I can do about it," if they, like him, think the moment near "when the sea of barbarism is about to break over us," and that before the disaster they should give themselves up in aristocratic aloofness to the contemplation of the greatness that is gone. They turn quietly away, uneasy at the public spectacle which is being enacted upon the German scene. Their voices are not heard in the land, but although they have isolated themselves and are scattered far apart, they assume, for all, the important task of guarding the threatened heritage of a great tradition, to preserve it for the time to come.

E. R. CURTIUS

VI

THE THREATENED HERITAGE

IT is difficult to estimate the effect of the Nazi decade upon German literature. No earlier form of absolutism had exercised so thoroughgoing and drastic a supervision of all aspects of the spiritual life. At no time in Germany or elsewhere had an entire body of widely read and rightly influential literature been forced to disappear and go into exile. That part of the literary life which, for better or for worse, maintained itself within the Reich submitted, of course, to the most complete ideological control imaginable. But it would, nevertheless, be absurd to suppose that during the authoritarian decade literature—significant literature—had altogether vanished or lost its function.

Undoubtedly many of the more agile literary figures adjusted their output without serious scruples to the inevitable climate. Among the lesser journalists, poets, and dramatists this attitude will be found not to have been uncommon. But it must at the same time be said that no small number of distinguished writers have continued, with or without the expressed approval of the authorities and in spite of the rigors of the time, to pursue their literary work. Strong intellectual currents, coming to life, as we have seen, long before the cataclysmic crisis of the thirties, have carried these men across the period of perilous suspense. By 1934 Rilke, Hofmannsthal, and George were no longer alive, but in their places men of a similar, though perhaps lesser poetic talent, were being seriously regarded. Some of the chief novelists, poets, and playwrights of the period (Stehr, Strauss, Schröder, Mell, even Gerhart Hauptmann), although they seemed only in a superficial sense in tune with the current ideology, were now, as if by an unexpected but well-deserved accident of history, pushed from the periphery of the literary scene into the foreground of attention. The intrinsic merit of some of these should not be questioned, and their work will not soon lose its distinction.

It is not easy to accept the artificial unanimity of subject matter in the literature of the thirties, and the persistent emphasis, not by any means upon the more spectacular conflicts of contemporary civilization or —as in much of Soviet fiction—upon the creative allegiance to an emerging proletarian order, but rather upon the simple pattern of an elementary life in nature. This concept of the natural life is, of course, fundamentally a vision of salvation which is to be substituted for the destroyed forms of the bourgeois order, and it may well be suggested that the contemporary German writer merely seizes, either voluntarily or under the compulsion of fascist thinking, upon a chimerical device. Instead of coping plausibly with the exigencies of a severe social dislocation, he seems often to escape into a romantic area of naïve, even irresponsible, speculation. But, especially in the light of the previous evidence, it should not be forgotten that the universal destruction of bourgeois tenets has struck the German with particular severity. Alienation from an inherently ordered life concerns him more deeply than it does others, since the foundations of his social and political existence have, throughout his history, been peculiarly insecure. At all points of crisis he has been inclined to turn radically to the resources of a hypothetical natural life, while other nations, fundamentally more confident of their social structure, have at times of similar stress been content with a gradual and reasoned modification of their disturbed equilibrium.

But there is one further thought to be emphasized: if to the modern western mind a "return to nature" has inevitably the connotation of unrealistic sentimentality and suggests a perverted repudiation of all elements of cultural living, it is not usually so with the German, whose concept and experience of nature is, in itself, essentially civilized and charged with a variety of social, historical, and religious memories. What to the outsider seems merely *schwärmerisch* and irrational is to the German a positive and supremely satisfying cultural attitude.

A preoccupation with nature, thus understood as accepting life not only within the desiccated limits of the city, but in a more loosely defined frame of elemental, though deeply civilized, obligations, is the avowed theme of much of that German literature which has sprung up in the antibourgeois, postbourgeois climate of the past ten years. Some, though not many, of the younger novelists have produced, even within the confines of this subject matter, works of independent and distinct value. Friedrich Griese (b. 1890), Karl Heinrich Waggerl (b. 1897), Ernst Wiechert (b. 1887), Ludwig Tügel (b. 1889), Karl Benno von Mechow (b. 1897), Paul Alverdes (b. 1897), and many others have written novels with that peculiar provincial and emotional strength which is inherent in the tradition of German fiction. But their work transcends the restricted confines of a neopastoral setting; where it promises to remain alive, it draws, paradoxically, on the literary substance and form of the past; it owes as much to memories of the serene and still coherent nineteenth-century world of Jean Paul Richter, Stifter, and Keller as it does to the ironic formal tradition from Flaubert to Hamsun and Thomas Mann.

Upon these writers two of the older novelists of major rank have continued to exercise a significant influence. Both Emil Strauss (b. 1866) and Hermann Stehr (1864–1940) elaborate many of the problems which occupied the preceding generation—their cultural criticism is not dogmatic but generously humanitarian, and their faith in the creative strength of certain individual and communal values separates them from the more radical political novel of the kind which Döblin achieved in his *Berlin Alexanderplatz.*

Strauss is one of the most pleasing narrative talents of the recent past; coming, like his less decisive contemporaries, Emil Gött (1864–1908) and Hermann Hesse, from the meditative and imaginative region of the southwest, he has in his thinking and craftsmanship much of the easy warmth and calm manner of Gottfried Keller. His prose is lyrical and careful, and the scope of his world is impressive; so delightful and singularly perfect a short story as *Der Engelwirt* (1901) or the delicate portrait of *Freund Hein* (1902), and the volume, *Hans und Grete* (1909), stand next to graver and broader social novels, *Der nackte Mann* (1912), *Das Riesenspielzeug* (1935), and *Lebenstanz* (1941), in which he is, perhaps, unduly forced in his argumentation and less successful than in the lighter tales.

Hermann Stehr belongs to a different and more hectic psychological climate; he is the most conspicuous example of that febrile, even mystical, kind of inspiration which has so often given a puzzling depth to the form and genius of the German novel. Ever since his first more naturalistic prose works, he has drawn upon the visionary strength of his Silesian temperament, akin, in some respects, to the troubled gravity in the novels of Gerhart Hauptmann's gifted brother, Carl (1858–1921). Again and again his conception of a dark and sorrow-laden life drove him to pitiless accounts of the deepest recesses of the human soul. Far removed from the fashionable tenets of contemporary psychoanalysis, he is, rather, concerned with the less explicit powers of a transcendent faith which is as fanatical as it is profound. In two magnificent trilogies (*Drei Nächte*, 1909, *Der Heiligenhof*, 1918, *Peter Brindeisener*, 1924, and *Nathanael Maechler*, 1929, *Die Nachkommen*, 1933, *Damian Maechler* [as yet unpublished]) he has created a rich and simple world of peasants and artisans, of farm, village, and small town, set against a Silesian or Westphalian landscape and charged with that tense and dramatic kind of religious seriousness which will be remembered from Gerhart Hauptmann's novel, *Der Narr in Christo Emanuel Quint* (1910). By his belief in the absolute and creative power of the human resolve, Stehr dissociated himself, of course, from the determinist attitude of his naturalistic contemporaries and became one of the cardinal and positive examples of the expressionist sensibility.

These and similarly tuned minor novelists (Wilhelm Schmidtbonn, b. 1876, Hermann Burte, b. 1879, Alfons Paquet, 1881–1943) achieve by their reference to regional and "natural" values a striking emotional vigor. At their best they are neither flatly provincial nor intellectually confined: the Alsatian, René

Schickele (1883–1940), for instance, who is delicate and expert in craftsmanship and at the same time rooted in his love of the Alemannic land, reaches pleadingly across the unhappy line which divides the cultures of the Rhine. Yet, Schickele is never narrowly patriotic, nor does he lose, even in his cosmopolitan essays (*Die Genfer Reise*, 1919, and *Liebe und Ärgernis des D. H. Lawrence*, 1934), the profound attachment to his native scene which is the subject of all his later work, especially of the drama, *Hans im Schnakenloch* (1915), the narrative trilogy, *Das Erbe am Rhein* (1925–1927), and *Himmlische Landschaft* (1932).

Rudolf Binding's (1867–1938) stories (*Legenden der Zeit*, 1909, *Die Geige*, 1911, *Unsterblichkeit*, 1922, and *Erlebtes Leben*, 1928) and the autobiographical tales of Hans Carossa point in another direction: together with the remarkable prose of Ernst Jünger and certain elements in Thomas Mann's work, from *Der Zauberberg* to his pointillist portrait of Goethe (*Lotte in Weimar*, 1939) and the most recent *Joseph* volumes (1933–1944), they are documents of a specifically humanistic concern for the moral and spiritual heritage. Binding's talent is, perhaps, essentially one of manner; his well-bred elegance and his verve find their expression in a literary style which is sure, firm, and, in spite of its deliberateness, never pretentious. His prose is chiseled but not cold; his language moves in a lucid, limpid stream; and an unfailing command of the light as well as the sombre mood lends variety to his short stories.

The dignified work of Hans Carossa (b. 1878) is less dazzling in character. He recounts in three slow-moving and tranquil volumes (*Eine Kindheit*, 1922, *Verwandlungen einer Jugend*, 1928, and *Das Jahr der schönen Täuschungen*, 1941) his early years in Bavaria; *Rumänisches Tagebuch* (1924) and *Führung und Geleit* (1933) survey certain aspects of his later life. In his first short story, *Doktor Bürgers Ende* (1913), and the beautifully balanced *Geheimnisse des reifen Lebens* (1936), he projects his own problematical experiences into an intermediate narrative figure. The famous address, *Wirkungen Goethes in der Gegenwart* (1938), focuses upon a great and radiant subject to which Carossa feels himself reverently drawn. *Der Arzt Gion* (1931), a novel of subdued colors and restrained psychological tensions, is his only objective piece of fiction. The generosity and wisdom of Carossa's temperament and his sympathy with all creative fully stylized; his poetry (*Gedichte*, 1910, 1929) aspects of life appear, in his prose, at times overcare-suffers less from the same occasional strain of formal effort; it succeeds in blending a tempered, Goethean idiom with elements of religious sensitiveness not unlike those of Gottfried Keller.

Although Carossa does not in a strict sense belong among them, a large number of pointedly Catholic writers have, during the past thirty years, been extraordinarily effective. The well-known work of Max Mell, Karl Heinrich Waggerl, and Richard Billinger rests, of course, like that of many others, on the splendid literary tradition of Austrian catholicism; but such excellent minor figures as Enrica von Handel-Mazzetti (b. 1871), Gertrud von Le Fort (b. 1876), Peter Dörfler (b. 1878), Paula Grogger (b. 1892) and Reinhold Schneider (b. 1903) have had their conspicuous share in the consolidation of German literature between the wars. Among the Catholic critics there have been distinguished contributors, not only to the general discussion of cultural issues, but to the field of specifically literary appreciation (Karl Muth, b. 1867, Theodor Haecker, b. 1879, Günther Müller, b. 1881, and Romano Guardini, 1885–1941).

Catholic and Protestant writers alike are preoccupied with the paradoxical human quest for both responsibility and freedom, a theme which is fundamental in the literature of our time and which has, in Germany, been stated and pursued most effectively, not in political terms, but rather in its wider religious context. It is in this ambit of peculiarly modern religious speculation that some of the contemporary German philosophers have exercised a remarkable influence upon the literature of Europe and America. It is characteristic of this form of religious thought to derive philosophical conclusions not so much from the dialectical manipulation of idealistic concepts as from the compelling implications, both rational and irrational, of the human situation. Religious philosophy in this "existential" sense is, once again, urgently concerned with questions of meaning and value. Historically, it draws not only upon Nietzsche but upon the newly relevant Protestant work of Søren Kierkegaard (1813–1855), and has found in contemporary psychologists, philosophers, and theologians, like Carl Gustav Jung, (b. 1875), Max Scheler (1874–1928), Karl Barth (b. 1886), Karl Jaspers (b. 1883), and Martin Heidegger (b. 1889), provocative expression.

Whatever the sources of the emotional cohesion which the contemporary writer hopes to establish, whether historical, regional, or religious, whether reasoned or irrational, the idiom of the past fifteen years is tranquil and collected. It conveys a calm which is not always free from strain and which is the evidence of a deep sense of renunciation. Its dominant character, in remarkable contrast to the experimental temper of the war generation, is a self-conscious obligation to tradition. Many of the historical attitudes of form and feeling have, therefore, persisted: it would not be difficult to point to impressionist or neorealist, naturalistic or symbolist qualities even in the poetry of the more distinguished modernists.

But it is, perhaps, possible, beyond these formal categories, to suggest summarily four distinct phases in the shifting of poetic perception since the last war. The first, more genuine and more radical than any other in contemporary European literature, produced the hyperbolical manner of the expressionists, of which something has been said earlier. But while these revolutionary poets dealt with problems of the social and political crisis in large and metaphysical gestures, many of their less militant contemporaries withdrew from a disappointing present deliberately and without even an indication of protest. The form of their work, different from the loose, sharp cry of the years of the First World War, was severe and their melody restrained. The poetry of the later Rilke, of Binding and Carossa, of Rudolf Borchardt (b. 1877) and Rudolf Alexander Schröder (b. 1878), of Oskar Loerke (1884–1941) and Agnes Miegel (b. 1879), and the singularly impressive epic poems of Albrecht Schaeffer (b. 1885) are all indicative of a palpable shift from expressionist abandon to the austerity of a disciplined idiom.

Not only R. A. Schröder's translations (Homer, 1910, Virgil, 1924, 1926, Racine, 1932, and Horace, 1935), but his volumes of sustained and cautiously designed poetry (*Lieder und Elegien,* 1911, *Deutsche Oden,* 1913, *Mitte des Lebens,* 1930, and *Die weltlichen Gedichte,* 1940) give him a secure place near Rudolf Borchardt, the most accomplished and circumspect of the formal poets of the present. Hardly disturbed by the passing fashions of the century, Borchardt has sought and rediscovered the highest examples of poetic responsibility in the spiritual traditions of western Europe and the Mediterranean. In spite of a passing association with George, there is in him more of the radiant and musical sensitiveness of Hofmannsthal (*Rede über Hofmannsthal,* 1905): in the grave and measured but incandescent elegance of his prose (*Prosa I,* 1924, and *Gespräch über Formen,* 1905), in the volumes of his short verse (*Jugendgedichte,* 1913, *Die Schöpfung aus Liebe,* 1923, and *Vermischte Gedichte,* 1924), and especially in the taut rhythms of his epic poem, *Der Durant* (1921), he has produced works unequaled for their mastery of language. Only a certain critical impatience will dismiss Borchardt's achievement as mere formalism. He realized, as few in his age have done, that form is the only criterion of literary greatness. It was his aim, not least in his translations of the Provençal poets (*Die grossen Trobadors,* 1924), of Dante (*Vita Nova,* 1922, and *Dante Deutsch,* 1930), and of Pindar (*Pindarische Gedichte,* 1931), to create a new and elevated medium of expression from the remoter sources of the German language.

A third and startling phase of the recent progress of poetry began with Bertolt Brecht's effective *Hauspostille* (1927) and developed its own characteristics in the catching and ironic *Gebrauchslyrik* of Erich Kästner (1899–1942, *Herz auf Taille,* 1928, *Lyrische Hausapotheke,* 1938), in Walter Mehring's (b. 1896) *Gedichte, Lieder und Chansons* (1929), and in the melancholy and reticent verses of Joachim Ringelnatz (1883–1934, *Gedichte dreier Jahre,* 1932, and *Ge-*

dichte, Gedichte, von einstmal und heute, 1934). These poets, in manner though not in content indebted to Christian Morgenstern (1871–1914), hoped for the response of a politically alert public. Elements of Villon and Kipling, of the popular ballad, street cries, and vaudeville are boldly compounded to expose the pathetic absurdity of the bourgeois life. By a radical use of everyday speech and amusingly sophisticated formal patterns, they aimed at producing what were called "quotable gestures," and thus reclaimed for the poet a specific function in the debate of pressing current issues. Whether they represented the ideology of right or left, they advanced, underneath their attitude of deceptive detachment, the strongest claim to political action.

The fourth and contemporary aspect owes its peculiar character first of all to a striking and not always organic change in subject matter—a change away from collective and liberal social themes towards the more irrational subject of man's place in the total natural frame of his earthly life. It is a poetry of being, and not of speculation or knowledge. This change must seem surprising at a moment when the constructive thinking of the time is focused more directly than ever before upon economic and social issues. But the discrepancy exists only on the surface, for the poet shares with the novelist the knowledge that, of all the spiritual conflicts which are common to contemporary literatures, the conflict between the increasing rationalization of living and the inescapable pressure of irrational impulses is the most serious. The German poet of the last decade sees this clearly, but instead of stating it in terms of urban social friction, he represents the individual within the less distinct but more comprehensive frame of nature.

This turn from a superficially modern type of subject matter to another of far less immediate actuality creates, of course, difficulties which are not merely formal: since the exigencies of the contemporary world do not easily lend themselves to either pastoral or irony, the German poet has resorted, with perhaps a large measure of self-conscious effort, to the heroic. But he is no longer content with the bareness of the poetic landscape of his immediate predecessors; he conceives of nature as lyrical and even demonic. He has abandoned the plaintive recording of his own disillusionment and now projects, with a resolute will to order, tentative patterns of existential coherence. In this revival of neoidealistic conventions, romantic and classicist elements are curiously interwoven. In present-day painting and in much of contemporary European music this return to themes and images of the early nineteenth century has often been observed. But it is no less striking in the work of the younger poets.

Where the new attitude does not simply resort to the common devices of secondhand romanticism (as it does in the popular verses of Ruth Schaumann,

b. 1899, and the older Hermann Claudius, b. 1878), but is, rather, coupled with genuine insight into the conditions of our technological civilization, it is likely to produce poetry of a distinctive style. Such conspicuous poets as the novelist's brother, Friedrich Georg Jünger (b. 1897, cf. his essay, *Illusionen der Technik*, 1940), and Fritz Usinger (b. 1895) represent this disciplined type of perception with extraordinary power. Moreover, Jünger's verse (*Gedichte*, 1934, and *Der Taurus*, 1937) and Usinger's *Die Stimmen* (1934) and *Die Geheimnisse* (1937) indicate a return to the larger and more demanding poetic forms. After the pungent and caustic short verses of the *Gebrauchslyriker*, the contemporary poets cultivate certain strenuous classical meters. Severe rhymed verses, hymns, odes, elegiac poems, choral chants, and, on a more popular level, the ballad have regained their function as astringent media of expression. Here and there the preoccupation with matters of design results in artificiality. The work, for instance, of so serious a poet as the Austrian, Josef Weinheber (b. 1892, *Adel und Untergang*, 1934, *Späte Krone*, 1936, and *Zwischen Göttern und Dämonen*, 1938) is, in spite of its unusually accurate sense of the stylized gesture, seldom relieved and hardly ever without a palpable strain.

Much of the recent poetry is objective, though not necessarily impersonal; it is "oftener prismatic than diaphanous" and owes its intensity of form, on the one hand, to the subtlety of Rilke's late elegies, and on the other to the widely admired pathos of Hölderlin, Germany's greatest pure poet. In these two commanding figures the modern poets recognize the most successful transformation of a supremely humanistic vision of nature into the most passionate and religious poetry.

It must seem perplexing that, at a time when such political pressure is brought upon the poet to force him to be useful as a propagandist, he should have deliberately concerned himself with matters of a distinctly formal nature. It is hardly sufficient to characterize—and dismiss—this not at all infrequent attitude as a mere escape from the spiritual discomforts of a brutal ideological climate into an aesthetic no man's land. We must, rather, assume that the devotion to the literary craft and the self-denying concentration upon the matter and manner of past greatness constitute acts of defiance which are as such of no small political significance.

Much of the enormous poetic output of the present is, naturally, of indifferent value. It would be unjust to deny a certain political effectiveness to such younger poets as Herybert Menzel (b. 1906), Herbert Böhme (b. 1907), and Gerhard Schumann (b. 1911). But most of these minor and ostentatious poets live only by the artificial inner—and outer—support of a rigid dogma. Their jejune work serves the demands of a brief day; not the limitations of subject matter alone but their blunt and defective perception will deprive them of permanent significance.

Something of the declamatoriness of the poets is also apparent in the more recent drama, for which the early expressionist, Hanns Johst (b. 1890, *Der junge Mensch*, 1916, and *Thomas Paine*, 1927), has been a vociferous, though by no means distinguished, spokesman. The combination of modern technical resources (radio, film, mass meeting, open-air stage) and an urgent sense of the dramatist's propagandistic function have produced a peculiar theatrical idiom in which strained solemnity alternates with palpable doctrine and broad popular appeal. Many of the devices of the immediate past, the irregular design of the expressionist drama and the harsh contrasts of the political theater, have survived the drastic change in intellectual purpose. At the same time, it is the dramatist, the literary artist, who has reclaimed his primacy over the theatrical *régisseur*. His effectiveness is, on the surface, greater than ever, for he can count upon an apparent uniformity of political experience and belief. This identity of attitude is, of course, to a large degree a totalitarian artifice, but its precarious presence has given to the playwright a semblance of purpose. Some of the older dramatists, Paul Ernst, Ernst Bacmeister (b. 1874), and Hermann Burte, have been brought into a position of new relevance. Their critical thinking, heightened by emotional premises which it is difficult for an outsider to grasp or share, has provoked a vigorous discussion of the contemporary function and form of the drama Curt Langenbeck (b. 1906) maintained in a widely discussed essay ("Die Wiedergeburt des Dramas aus dem Geist der Zeit," 1940) the possibility of a secular tragedy in the spirit not of the analytical and individualistic Shakespeare but of the Greeks. Here, as among the poets, it is the gesture of human defiance—and not salvation—in the face of natural and recognized limitations which, once again, makes certain lofty dramatic effects plausible.

The subject matter of the new drama, not unlike that of the novel, is, of course, tied to the oppressive experiences of the decade. But it does not commonly appear in the direct use of present-day themes. Indeed, historical settings predominate. Hans Schwarz (b. 1890, *Rebell in England*, 1934, and *Prinz von Preussen*, 1934), Eberhard Wolfgang Möller (b. 1906, *Frankenburger Würfelspiel*, 1936, and *Der Sturz des Ministers*, 1937), and Gerhard Menzel (b. 1894, *Toboggan*, 1928, *Scharnhorst*, 1935) have written plays with a strong and Protestant emphasis upon the political duties of the individual, and with careful—even forced—attention to the effects of language.

The same interest in the resonance and strength of dramatic speech is evident in many of the recent radio plays, such as Richard Euringer's (b. 1891) early *Deutsche Passion 1933* (1933), Möller's *Der Soldatenkönig* (1936), and Josef Martin Bauer's (b. 1901) *Das tote Herz* (1939). But a comparison with some of the distinguished English and American broadcast ballads shows the dangers which lie in the unrelieved use of an artificial pathos.

A fine and natural concern for the effects of the poetic word has given peculiar distinction to the writings of Richard Billinger (b. 1893) and Max Mell (b. 1882), both Austrians, whose lyrical force (Mell's *Gedichte*, 1929, and Billinger's *Nachtwache*, 1935) adds value to their cautious but substantial dramatic talents. Billinger is of the two the more direct; his plays (*Das Perchtenspiel*, 1928, *Rauhnacht*, 1931, and *Der Gigant*, 1937) paraphrase with the brusque accents of the ballad the common and somber themes of life among the peasants. Mell's art is more delicately filtered and refined; his prose (*Das Donauweibchen*, 1938, and *Steirischer Lobgesang*, 1940) has the melodious realism of Carossa and the quiet serenity of Adalbert Stifter. Several of his playlets, especially *Das Apostelspiel* (1923), *Das Schutzengelspiel* (1923), *Das Nachfolge-Christi-Spiel* (1927), and *Das Spiel von den deutschen Ahnen* (1935), although endowed with subtle and deliberate elements of modernity, rest upon the spiritual tradition of the Austro-Catholic mystery drama which Hugo von Hofmannsthal had recently revived.

Many of the German writers whose work reflected and illuminated the European world between 1914 and 1934 are now abroad, cut off from the immediate response without which genuine creative work is impossible, but still in most cases vigorously prepared to defend a purer image of the life from which they were compelled to part. The poisoned torrents of indoctrination and propaganda have often enough washed aside much of their past reputation and perhaps no little of their future effectiveness; for in the meantime they have sought a new, and, as they hope, permanent sphere of work. The older and once established artists, Heinrich and Thomas Mann, Werfel, Schaeffer, Herrmann-Neisse, Beer-Hofmann, Döblin, Unruh, Bruno Frank, Arnold Zweig, may find the relevance of their work seriously reduced. Many have gone through concentration camps and years of the deepest despair; some, Hasenclever, Toller, and Stefan Zweig, have ended their own lives.

A few of the younger authors, Becher, Brecht, Graf, Hauser, Kesten, Klaus Mann, Renn, Seghers, Zuckmayer, and others, have adjusted themselves, in Russia, the Americas, or England, with a large measure of success, to the compulsion of new languages, new idioms, and new literary practices. Fresh talents have emerged among the novelists and have taken their place in the ranks of a supremely militant generation. With enterprise and intelligence, German literary magazines abroad (*Mass und Wert, Die Sammlung, Das Wort, Deutsche Blätter,* and others) have carried the will and vision of the exiled across more than ten years of enforced separation.

Pledged to the image of free men, these writers, young or old, will contribute in due course to the determined features of the European artist, hardened in an age which is unprecedented in its suffering but unsurpassed in courage and decision. If fear and guilt, weakness and indulgence, uncertainty and speculation have been the element of much of Europe's recent literature, the years to come will challenge the poet—whatever his language or his symbols—to reassert, against the evidence of incoherence and destruction, his destined power of evoking and sustaining the permanent signs of human virtue and resolution.

BIBLIOGRAPHY AND INDEXES

BIBLIOGRAPHY

THE following bibliography includes not only a selected number of general studies in English dealing with the period under discussion, but lists as fully as possible the translated works, since 1870, of the imaginative writers named in the text. In the case of several authors, especially those whose works belong to the earlier decades, it has been thought advisable, for reasons of economy, not to repeat the information given in B. Q. Morgan's *Critical Bibliography of German Literature in English Translation* (2d ed., 1938). In each such instance specific reference is made to Morgan's list, which is frequently supplemented by additional items.

From the philosophers and historians, only certain conspicuous titles have been included.

As a rule, only the most accessible publications are cited, even though several other translations of the same work may have appeared.

In the brief references to critical and biographical articles on individual authors, no mention is made of encyclopedic works, such as *Current Biography, Dictionary of Modern European Literature,* and *Twentieth-Century Authors.* When reference is made, under the individual authors, to a work listed in one of the first three sections of this bibliography, full data are not given for that work in the fourth section.

BIBLIOGRAPHY

GERMANY AND THE GERMANS

Bithell, J., ed. *Germany, a Companion to German Studies.* 3d ed. London, Methuen, 1942.

Brock, W. *Introduction to Contemporary German Philosophy.* Cambridge, [Eng.], University Press, 1935.

Diesel, E. *Germany and the Germans.* New York, Macmillan, 1931.

Fife, R. H. *The German Empire Between Two Wars; a Study of the Political and Social Development of the Nation Between 1871 and 1914.* New York, Macmillan, 1916.

Herford, C. H. *The Post-War Mind of Germany.* Oxford, Clarendon Press, 1927.

Johnson, F. *The German Mind as Reflected in Their Literature from 1870 to 1914.* London, Chapman & Dodd, 1922.

Jones, W. T. *Contemporary Thought of Germany.* London, Williams & Norgate, 1930–31. 2 vols.

Pinnow, H. *History of Germany.* Rev. ed. London, Dent, 1939.

Scheffauer, H. G. *The New Vision in the German Arts.* New York, Huebsch, 1924.

Schuman, F. L. *Germany Since 1918.* New York, Holt, 1937.

Schuster, G. N., and A. Bergstraesser. *Germany, a Short History.* New York, Norton, 1944.

Steinberg, S. H. *A Short History of Germany.* Cambridge, [Eng.], University Press, 1944.

Thoene, P. *Modern German Art.* London, Penguin Books, 1938.

Vermeil, E. *Germany's Three Reichs.* London, Dakers, 1944.

Viereck, P. R. E. *Metapolitics; from the Romantics to Hitler.* New York, Knopf, 1941.

HISTORY OF GERMAN LITERATURE

BOOKS

Bennett, E. K. *A History of the German Novelle from Goethe to Thomas Mann.* Cambridge, [Eng.], University Press, 1934.

Bertaux, F. *Panorama of German Literature from 1871 to 1931.* New York, Whittlesey House, 1935.

Bettex, A. W. *The German Novel of To-day.* Cambridge, [Eng.], Bowes & Bowes, 1939.

Bithell, J. *Modern German Literature, 1880–1938.* London, Methuen, 1939.

Bostock, J. K. *Some Well-known German War Novels, 1914–1930.* Oxford, Blackwell, 1931.

Butler, E. M. *The Tyranny of Greece over Germany.* Cambridge, [Eng.], University Press, 1935.

Closs, A. *The Genius of the German Lyric.* London, Allen & Unwin, 1938.

Eloesser, A. *Modern German Literature.* New York, Knopf, 1933.

Hentschel, C. *The Byronic Teuton, Aspects of German Pessimism, 1800–1933.* London, Methuen, 1940.

Hewett-Thayer, H. W. *The Modern German Novel.* Boston, Marshall Jones Co., 1924.

Kaufmann, F. W. *German Dramatists of the 19th Century.* Los Angeles, Calif., Lymanhouse, 1940.

Klenze, C. von. *From Goethe to Hauptmann; Studies in a Changing Culture.* New York, Viking Press, 1926.

Kohn-Bramstedt, E. *Aristocracy and the Middle Classes in Germany; Social Types in German Literature, 1830–1900.* London, P. S. King, 1937.

Lessing, O. E. *Masters in Modern German Literature.* Dresden, Reissner, 1912.

Lewisohn, L. *The Spirit of Modern German Literature.* New York, Huebsch, 1916.

Liptzin, S. *Germany's Stepchildren.* Philadelphia, The Jewish Publication Society, 1944.

Liptzin, S. *Lyric Pioneers of Modern Germany; Studies in German Social Poetry.* New York, Columbia Univ. Press, 1928.

Pfeiler, W. K. *War and the German Mind; the Testimony of Men of Fiction Who Fought at the Front.* New York, Columbia Univ. Press, 1941.

Rose, W. *Men, Myths, and Movements in German Literature.* London, Allen & Unwin, 1931.

Rose, W., ed. *Contemporary Movements in European Literature.* London, Routledge & Sons, 1928.

Samuel, R., and R. H. Thomas. *Expressionism in German Life, Literature, and the Theatre (1910–1924).* Cambridge, [Eng.], Heffer & Sons, 1939.

Slochower, H. *No Voice Is Wholly Lost.* New York, Creative Age Press, 1945.

Stirk, S. D. *The Prussian Spirit, a Survey of German Literature and Politics, 1914–1940.* London, Faber & Faber, 1941.

Thomas, R. H. *German Perspectives; Essays on German Literature.* Cambridge, [Eng.], Heffer & Sons, 1940.

PERIODICAL ARTICLES

Aron, A. W. "Some Tendencies in the Modern German Ballad," *Philological Quarterly,* VI (1928), 270–276.

Bentley, E. R. "German Writers in Exile, 1933–1943," *Books Abroad,* XVII (1943), 313–317.

Deutsch, B. "A Note on Modern German Poetry," *Poetry,* XXI (1922), 149–153.

Douglass, P. "Literature in the Third Reich," *Books Abroad,* VIII (1934), 384–386.

Dukes, A. "The Scene in Europe: Nazi Theatre," *Theatre Arts Monthly,* XVIII (1934), 21–32; XIX (1935), 177–184.

Evans, G. "Towards a New Drama in Germany; a Survey of the Years 1933–1937," *German Life and Letters,* II (1937–38), 188–200.

Hirsch, F. E. "Recent Historical Writing in Germany," *Books Abroad,* XI (1937), 3–7.

Hodsoll, E. R. "German Literature To-day," *Contemporary Review,* CLV (1939), 709–716.

Kollmann, E. C. "Characteristics of Austrian Literature," *Monatshefte für deutschen Unterricht,* XXXIV (1942), 307–317.

Lawson, M. F. "Trends in Recent German Literature," *Monatshefte für deutschen Unterricht*, XXVIII (1936), 49–59.

Lissau, R. "Recent Austrian Literature," *German Life and Letters*, IV (1939), 35–45.

Mankiewicz, F. "German Literature, 1933–1938," *German Quarterly*, XII (1939), 179–191.

Neuse, W. "Poetry in the Third Reich," *Books Abroad*, XII (1938), 14–16.

Paulsen, W. "The Foundations of Modern German Literature," *Durham University Journal*, June, 1936.

Peacock, R. "The Great War in German Lyrical Poetry, 1914–1918," *Leeds Philosophical Society, Proceedings of the Literary and Historical Section*, III (1934), 189–243.

Randall, A. W. G. "Contemporary German Dramatists," *Dial*, LXXI (1921), 172–178.

Randall, A. W. G. "The Neo-classic Movement in 20th-Century German Drama," *New Europe*, XIII (1919–20), 219–223.

Randall, A. W. G. "The Spirit of Contemporary German Literature," *London Mercury*, VII (1922–23), 46–53.

Reinhardt, K. F. "The Expressionist Movement in Recent German Literature," *Germanic Review*, VI (1931), 256–265.

Roger-Henrichsen, G. "German Refugee Literature," *London Mercury*, XXXIX (1939), 402–408.

Rose, W. "Contemporary German Literature: the Younger Generation," *London Mercury*, XVI (1927), 512–524.

Scheffauer, E. T. "Some German Post-War Lyric Poets," *Poetry Review*, XXVIII (1937), 205–221.

Schnitzler, H. "Some Remarks on Austrian Literature," *Books Abroad*, XVII (1943), 215–221.

Schumann, D. W. "Expressionism and Post-Expressionism in German Lyrics," *Germanic Review*, IX (1934), 54–66, 115–129.

Schumann, D. W. "Motifs of Cultural Eschatology in German Poetry from Naturalism to Expressionism," *PMLA*, LVIII (1943), 1125–1177.

Smith, M. J. "Between Two Worlds; the Artist and Society in the

Modern German Novel," *Modern Languages,* XIV (1933), 175–184.

Wadsworth, P. B. "The Young Writers of Germany," *Bookman* (N.Y.), LXXV (1932), 260–268.

Wassermann, J. "Tendencies of the Modern German Novel," *Fortnightly Review,* CXLI (1934), 60–68.

Weiskopf, F. C. "Bitter Bread, Exiled German Writers in the Belligerent Countries," *Books Abroad,* XIV (1940), 252–257.

Zabel, M. D. "The New Poets of Germany," *Poetry,* XXXIV (1929), 94–99.

ANTHOLOGIES OF GERMAN LITERATURE IN ENGLISH TRANSLATION

Bennett, E. N., ed. *German Short Stories.* London, Oxford Univ. Press, 1934.

Bern, M., comp. *The German Lyric Since Goethe.* Paris, Hachette, 1926.

Bithell, J., comp. *Contemporary German Poetry.* London, Walter Scott Pub. Co., 1909.

Broicher, D. *German Lyrists of Today.* London, Mathews, 1912.

Busch, M., tr. *Selected Austrian Short Stories.* London, Oxford Univ. Press, 1929.

Cerf, B. A., ed. *Great German Short Stories and Novels.* New York, Modern Library, 1933.

Crippen, H. R., ed. *Germany: a Self-Portrait; a Collection of German Writings from 1914 to 1943.* London, Oxford Univ. Press, 1944.

Deutsch, B., and A. Yarmolinsky, ed. *Contemporary German Poetry; an Anthology.* New York, Harcourt, Brace, 1923.

Francke, K., ed. *German Classics of the XIX and XX Centuries.* New York, German Publication Society, 1913–15. 20 vols.

Mann, K., and H. Kesten, eds. *Heart of Europe; an Anthology of*

Creative Writing in Europe, 1920–1940. New York, Fischer, 1943.

Münsterberg, M., comp. *A Harvest of German Verse.* New York, Appleton, 1916.

Rothensteiner, J. E. *A German Garden of the Heart.* St. Louis, Herder Book Co., 1934.

Steinhauer, H., and H. Jessiman, trs. *Modern German Short Stories.* London, Oxford Univ. Press, 1938.

Van Doren, M. *An Anthology of World Poetry.* New York, Literary Guild of America, 1928. pp. 902–928.

BIBLIOGRAPHIES OF GERMAN LITERATURE TRANSLATED INTO ENGLISH

Hansen, A. C. *Twentieth Century Forces in European Fiction.* Chicago, American Library Assoc., 1934.

Morgan, B. Q. *A Critical Bibliography of German Literature in English Translation.* 2d ed. Stanford University, Calif., University Press, 1938.

INDIVIDUAL AUTHORS

ALVERDES, PAUL

Der Nebenmann, 1927. Eng. tr., "Man in the Next Bed," in *Best Short Stories of the War,* New York, Harper, 1931.

Die Pfeiferstube, 1929. Eng. tr., *The Whistlers' Room,* New York, Covici-Friede, 1930.

Reinhold oder die Verwandelten, 1931. Eng. tr., *Reinhold, or the Transformed,* London, Secker, 1932. (1933 ed., *Changed Men.*)

BAHR, HERMANN

Der arme Narr, 1905. Eng. tr., "The Poor Fool," in *One-Act Plays Monthly,* II (1938), 3–33.

Expressionismus, 1916. Eng. tr., *Expressionism*, London, Henderson, 1925.

Das Konzert, 1909. Eng. tr., "The Concert," in Dickinson, T. H., ed., *Chief Contemporary Dramatists*, 2d ser., New York, Harcourt, Brace, 1921.

Der Meister, 1903. Eng. tr., *The Master*, Philadelphia, N. L. Brown, 1918.

Die schöne Frau, 1899. Eng. tr., "His Beautiful Wife," in Busch, *Selected Austrian Short Stories*.

REFERENCES

Drake, W. A., *Contemporary European Writers*, New York, Day, 1928, pp. 184–191.

Macken, M., "Hermann Bahr, His Personality and His Works," *Studies* (Dublin), XV (1926), 34–46, 573–586.

BARLACH, ERNST

REFERENCES

Dresdner, A., "Ernst Barlach," *Studio*, XCII (1926), 338–342.

Hauch, E. T., "Ernst Barlach and the Search for God," *Germanic Review*, II (1927), 157–166.

Mann, T., "German Letter," *Dial*, LXXVII (1924), 414–416.

BARTH, KARL

REFERENCES

Chapman, J. A., *The Theology of Karl Barth, a Short Introduction*, London, Epworth, 1931.

Demant, V. A., "Karl Barth and the Religious Situation," *Nineteenth Century*, CXXV (1939), 592–599.

Horton, W. M., *Contemporary Continental Theology*, New York, Harper, 1938, pp. 97–113.

Mackintosh, H. R., *Types of Modern Theology*, New York, Scribner's, 1937, pp. 263–319.

BECHER, JOHANNES ROBERT

Murder in Camp Hohenstein . . . (with other authors), London, Lawrence, 1933.

"The Resounding House," in *International Literature* (Moscow), 1934, no. 6, 57–67.

SELECTIONS

Crippen, *Germany.*

Davidman, J., ed., *War Poems of the United Nations,* New York, Dial Press, 1943.

Deutsch and Yarmolinsky, *Contemporary German Poetry.*

International Literature (Moscow), 1938, no. 6, pp. 62–64; 1940, no. 4–5, pp. 70–71; 1940, no. 8–9, pp. 90–93; 1942, no. 1–2, pp. 12–14, 68.

BEER-HOFMANN, RICHARD

Gedenkrede auf Mozart, 1906. Eng. tr., "Memorial Oration on Wolfgang Amadeus Mozart," in Mann and Kesten, *Heart of Europe.*

Der Graf von Charolais, 1905. Partial Eng. tr. in *This Quarter* (Paris), II (1931), no. 3.

Schlaflied für Miriam, 1898. Eng. tr., "Lullaby for Miriam," in *Poet Lore,* XLVII (1941), 290.

REFERENCE

Liptzin, S., *Richard Beer-Hofmann,* New York, Bloch Pub. Co., 1936.

BENN, GOTTFRIED

Gehirne, 1916. Excerpts tr.: "Island," in Jolas, E., ed., *Transition Stories,* New York, McFee, 1929. "The Birthday," in *Transition,* no. 5 (1927), 32–44.

SELECTIONS

Transition, no. 21 (1932), 107–112, 195–205; no. 23 (1935), 145–146.

REFERENCE

Jolas, E., "Gottfried Benn," *Transition,* no. 5 (1927), 146–147.

BILLINGER, RICHARD

REFERENCE

Hofmannsthal, H. von, "Vienna Letter," *Dial,* LXXVI (1924), 529–534.

BINDING, RUDOLF GEORG

Aus dem Kriege, 1925. Eng. tr., *A Fatalist at War,* London, Allen & Unwin, 1933.

Coelestina, 1908. Eng. tr., same title, in Steinhauer and Jessiman, *Modern German Short Stories.*

Der Wingult, 1921. Eng. tr., "Wingult," in *Best Short Stories of the War,* New York, Harper, 1931.

BLUNCK, HANS FRIEDRICH

"Auf dem Babenhof" (from *Gesammelte Werke,* 1937, Vol. V). Eng. tr., "On the Farm," in Maugham, W. S., ed., *Tellers of Tales,* New York, Doubleday, Doran, 1939.

BORCHARDT, RUDOLF

REFERENCE

Caffrey, G., "Rudolf Borchardt," *New Criterion,* V (1927), 81–87.

BRECHT, BERTOLT

Dreigroschenroman, 1934. Eng. tr., *A Penny for the Poor,* London, R. Hale, 1937.

"The Fourth Wall of China," in *Life and Letters To-day,* XV (1936), 116–123.

Gedichte aus dem Exil. Eng. tr., *Poems in Exile,* in *Kenyon Review,* VIII (1945), 198–207.

Die Gewehre der Frau Carrar, 1938. Eng. tr., "Señora Carrar's Rifles," in *Theatre Workshop,* II (1938), 30–50.

"The Informer," in *Living Age,* CCCLV (1938–39), 35–42.

"Jewish Wife," in *Nation,* CLVII (1943), 299–300.

Kalkutta, 4. Mai (with L. Feuchtwanger). Eng. tr., "Warren Hastings," in Feuchtwanger, L., *Two Anglo-Saxon Plays,* New York, Viking Press, 1928.

"Mother Courage," in *New Directions in Prose and Poetry, 1941,* Norfolk, Conn., New Directions, 1941.

Private Life of the Master Race, Norfolk, Conn., New Directions, 1944.

Die Rundköpfe und die Spitzköpfe, 1935. Eng. tr., "Round Head, Peak Head," in *International Literature* (Moscow), 1937, no. 5, 3–59.

Das Verhör des Lukullus, 1940. Eng. tr., *Trial of Lucullus,* New York, New Directions, 1943.

"Yes, I'm Going Away," in *Living Age*, CCCLVI (1939), 238–242.

SELECTIONS

Davidman, J., ed., *War Poems of the United Nations*, New York, Dial Press, 1943.

REFERENCES

Bryher, "Bertolt Brecht," *Life and Letters To-day*, XXXIII (1942), 97–103.

Gorelik, M., *New Theatres for Old*, New York, French, 1940.

Greenberg, C., "Bertolt Brecht's Poetry," *Partisan Review*, VIII (1941), 114–127.

Mann, T., "German Letter," *Dial*, LXXVII (1924), 416–419.

Thompson, L., "Bert Brecht," *Kenyon Review*, II (1940), 319–329.

Tretyakov, S., "Bert Brecht," *International Literature* (Moscow), 1937, no. 5, 60–70.

White, E. W., "Bertolt Brecht," *Life and Letters To-day*, XIII (1935), 65–76.

BREHM, BRUNO

Apis und Este, 1931. Eng. tr., *They Call it Patriotism*, Boston, Little, Brown, 1932.

Das war das Ende, 1932. Eng. tr., *That Was the End*, London, Hurst, 1934.

BROCH, HERMANN

"Adolf Hitler's Farewell Address," in *Saturday Review of Literature*, XXVII (Oct. 21, 1944), 5–8.

The Bewitchment [in progress]. Excerpt, "Introduction to a Peasant Novel," in Mann and Kesten, *Heart of Europe*.

Die Schlafwandler, 1931–32. Eng. tr., *The Sleepwalkers*, Boston, Little, Brown, 1932.

Der Tod des Vergil, 1945. Eng. tr., *The Death of Virgil*, New York, Pantheon Books, 1945.

Die unbekannte Grösse, 1933. Eng. tr., *The Unknown Quantity*, New York, Viking Press, 1935.

REFERENCES

Lehner, F., "Hermann Broch," *Life and Letters To-day*, XV (1936), 64–71.

Muir, E., "Hermann Broch," *Bookman* (New York), LXXV (1932), 664–668.

BRÖGER, KARL

Bunker 17, 1929. Eng. tr., *Pillbox 17*, London, Butterworth, 1930.

BRONNEN, ARNOLT

O.S., 1929. Eng. tr., S.O.S., London, Secker, 1930.

BRUCKNER, FERDINAND (i.e., Theodor Tagger)

Elisabeth von England, 1930. Eng. tr., *Elizabeth of England, a Legend*, London, Benn, 1931.

Die Rassen, 1933. Eng. tr., *The Races*, New York, Knopf, 1934.

"Self-Bondage," in Crippen, *Germany*.

BUSCH, WILHELM

(For translations see Morgan's *Critical Bibliography*, pp. 80–82, 700.)

CAROSSA, HANS

Der Arzt Gion, 1931. Eng. tr., *Dr. Gion*, New York, Ballou, 1933.

Eine Kindheit, 1922. Eng. tr., *A Childhood*, New York, Cape & Smith, 1932.

Rumänisches Tagebuch, 1924. Eng. tr., *Roumanian Diary*, New York, Knopf, 1930.

Verwandlungen einer Jugend, 1928. Eng. tr., *Boyhood and Youth*, New York, Brewer, Warren & Putnam, 1932.

REFERENCES

Baier, C., "Hans Carossa and the New Germany," *German Life and Letters*, III (1939), 125–137.

Bithell, J., in Carossa, H., *Eine Kindheit*, Oxford, Blackwell, 1942.

Frey, J. R., "The Function of the Writer; a Study in the Literary Theory of Carossa . . . ," *Monatshefte für deutschen Unterricht*, XXXII (1940), 266–278.

Hofrichter, R. J., *Three Poets and Reality*, New Haven, Yale Univ. Press, 1942, pp. 9–41.

Muir, E., "A Note on Hans Carossa," *Bookman* (New York), LXXII (1930–31), 404–408.

Peacock, R., "Carossa," *German Life and Letters*, II (1938), 217–225.

DÄUBLER, THEODOR

SELECTIONS

Deutsch and Yarmolinsky, *Contemporary German Poetry*.

DAUTHENDEY, MAX

REFERENCE

Wendt, H. G., *Max Dauthendey, Poet and Philosopher*, New York, Columbia Univ. Press, 1936.

DEHMEL, RICHARD

SELECTIONS

Bithell, *Contemporary German Poetry*.

Coxwell, C. F., *German Poetry*, London, C. W. Daniel Co., 1938.

Deutsch and Yarmolinsky, *Contemporary German Poetry*.

Francke, *German Classics*, Vol. XVIII.

Münsterberg, *Harvest of German Verse*.

Poet Lore, XXXI (1920), 401–421.

Van Doren, *Anthology of World Poetry*.

REFERENCES

Bruns, F., *Modern Thought in the German Lyric Poets*, Madison, Wis., Univ. of Wisconsin, 1921, pp. 86–101.

Drake, W. A., *Contemporary European Writers*, New York, Day, 1928, pp. 324–333.

House, R. T., "The Life and Poetry of Richard Dehmel," *Poet Lore*, XXXVIII (1927), 264–268.

Lessing, *Masters in Modern German Literature*, pp. 63–85.

Lewisohn, L., *Cities and Men*, New York, Harper, 1927, pp. 111–120.

Slochower, H., "Richard Dehmel and Our Age," *Germanic Review*, II (1927), 320–333.

DILTHEY, WILHELM

SELECTIONS

Lewisohn, L., *Modern Book of Criticism,* New York, Boni & Liveright, 1919.

REFERENCES

Goebel, J., "Wilhelm Dilthey and the Source of Literary History," *Journal of English and Germanic Philology,* XXVI (1926), 145–156.

Hodges, H. A., *Wilhelm Dilthey, an Introduction,* London, Oxford Univ. Press, 1944.

Wirth, O., *Wilhelm Scherer, Josef Nadler, and Wilhelm Dilthey as Literary Historians,* dissertation, Univ. of Chicago, 1938.

DÖBLIN, ALFRED

Berlin Alexanderplatz, 1929. Eng. tr., *Alexanderplatz, Berlin, the Story of Franz Biberkopf,* New York, Viking Press, 1931.

"Der Chefarzt" (Chapter XI of *Bürger und Soldaten, 1918,* 1939). Eng. tr., "The Chief," in Mann and Kesten, *Heart of Europe.*

Pardon wird nicht gegeben, 1935. Eng. tr., *Men Without Mercy,* London, Gollancz, 1937.

REFERENCES

Beach, J. W., *The Twentieth-Century Novel,* New York, Century Co., 1932, pp. 512–515.

Hofe, H. von, "German Literature in Exile: Alfred Döblin," *German Quarterly,* XVII (1944), 28–31.

Slochower, H., "Franz Werfel and Alfred Döblin," *Journal of English and Germanic Philology,* XXXIII (1934), 103–112.

DWINGER, EDWIN ERICH

Armee hinter Stacheldraht, 1929. Eng. tr., *Prisoners of War,* New York, Knopf, 1930. (British ed., *The Army Behind Barbed Wire.*)

Zwischen Weiss und Rot, 1930. Eng. tr., *Between White and Red,* New York, Scribner's, 1932.

REFERENCE

Pfeiler, *War and the German Mind,* pp. 280–285.

EBNER-ESCHENBACH, MARIE von

Der Fink, 1895. Eng. tr., "The Finch," in Busch, *Selected Austrian Short Stories.*

Jakob Szela, 1883. Eng. tr., same title, in Busch, *Selected Austrian Short Stories.*

(For other translations see Morgan's *Critical Bibliography,* p. 102.)

REFERENCE

O'Connor, E. M., *Marie Ebner,* London, Palmer, 1928.

EDSCHMID, KASIMIR

"Das beschämende Zimmer" (from *Das rasende Leben,* 1916). Eng. tr., "The Humiliating Room," in *Transition,* no. 14 (1928), 241–253.

Glanz und Elend Süd-Amerikas, 1931. Eng. tr., *South America, Lights and Shadows,* New York, Viking Press, 1932.

Lord Byron, Roman einer Leidenschaft, 1929. Eng. tr., *A Passionate Rebel, the Life of Lord Byron,* New York, Boni, 1930. (A different tr., *Lord Byron, the Story of a Passion,* London, Toumlin, 1930.)

ERNST, PAUL

"Ehe und Proletarisierung" (from Keyserling, H. von, *Das Ehe-Buch,* 1925). Eng. tr., "Marriage and Proletarianism," in Keyserling, H. von, *Book of Marriage,* New York, Harcourt, Brace, 1926.

Die Geliebte des Anderen, 1925. Eng. tr., "Beloved of the Other," in *Fortnightly Review,* CXXXI (1929), 277–287.

Der Hecht. Eng. tr., "The Pike," in Steinhauer and Jessiman, *Modern German Short Stories.*

REFERENCES

Cunningham, K., "Paul Ernst's Theory of the Novelle," in *German Studies Presented to H. G. Fiedler,* Oxford, Clarendon Press, 1938, pp. 125–144.

Gorr, A. C., "Paul Ernst and Classicism," *German Quarterly,* XVII (1944), 135–144.

Klenze, H. von, "Paul Ernst," *Books Abroad,* XV (1940), 30–35.

Meessen, H. J., "Paul Ernst's Transition from the Drama to the Epic," *Monatshefte für deutschen Unterricht,* XXXIII (1941), 163–171.

EURINGER, RICHARD

Fliegerschule 4, 1929. Eng. tr., "Flying School, 1914," in *Best Short Stories of the War,* New York, Harpers, 1931.

FALLADA, HANS (i.e., Rudolf Ditzen)

Altes Herz geht auf die Reise, 1936. Eng. tr., *An Old Heart Goes A-Journeying,* New York, Simon & Schuster, 1936.

Der eiserne Gustav, 1938. Eng. tr., *Iron Gustav,* London, Putnam, 1940.

Ich bekomme Arbeit, 1932. Eng. tr., "I Find Work," in Steinhauer and Jessiman, *Modern German Short Stories.*

Kleiner Mann, was nun? 1932. Eng. tr., *Little Man, What Now?* New York, Grosset & Dunlap, 1934.

Märchen vom Stadtschreiber der aufs Land flog, 1925. Eng. tr., *Sparrow Farm,* New York, Putnam, 1938.

Wer einmal aus dem Blechnapf frisst, 1934. Eng. tr., *The World Outside,* New York, Simon & Schuster, 1934. (British ed., *Who Eats Out of the Tin Bowl.*)

Wir hatten mal ein Kind, 1934. Eng. tr., *Once We Had a Child,* New York, Simon & Schuster, 1936.

Wolf unter Wölfen, 1937. Eng. tr., *Wolf Among Wolves,* New York, Putnam, 1938.

REFERENCES

Slochower, H., "Hauptmann and Fallada: Unco-ordinated Writers of Nazi Germany," *Accent,* III (1942), 18–25.

Wuk, H. A., "Hans Fallada," *Living Age,* CCCXLIV (1933), 328–332.

FONTANE, THEODOR

Bilderbuch aus England, 1860. Eng. tr., *Journeys to England in Victoria's Early Days,* London, Massie, 1939.

Effi Briest, 1895. Eng. tr., same title, in Francke, *German Classics,* Vol. XII.

Irrungen, Wirrungen, 1888. Eng. tr., "Trials and Tribulations," in *Harvard Classics, Shelf of Fiction,* New York, Collier, 1917.

Der Karrenschieber von Grisselsbrunn, 1885. Eng. tr., "Barrowman of Griffelsbrunn" [*sic*], in *Masterpiece Library of Short Stories,* London, Educational Book Co., [n.d.], Vol. XVII.

Wohin? 1888. Eng. tr., "Whither?" in *Masterpiece Library of Short Stories,* London, Educational Book Co., [n.d.], Vol. XVII.

REFERENCES

Davis, A. L., "Fontane as a Political Thinker," *Germanic Review,* VIII (1933), 183–194.

Hayens, K., *Theodor Fontane, a Critical Study,* London, W. Collins, 1920.

Hewett-Thayer, *Modern German Novel,* pp. 26–66.

Park, R., "Theodor Fontane's Unheroic Heroes," *Germanic Review,* XIV (1939), 32–44.

Shears, L. A., "Theodor Fontane as a Critic of the Novel," *PMLA,* XXXVIII (1923), 389–400.

FRANK, BRUNO

Cervantes, 1934. Eng. tr., *A Man Called Cervantes,* New York, Viking Press, 1935.

Ehre Vater und Mutter, 1942. Eng. tr., "Honor Thy Father and Thy Mother," in Robinson, A. L., ed., *The Ten Commandments,* New York, Simon & Schuster, 1943.

Der Goldene, 1920. Eng. tr., "The Golden Beetle," in Maugham, W. S., ed., *Tellers of Tales,* New York, Doubleday, Doran, 1939.

Der Handkoffer, 1920. Eng. tr., "The Suitcase," in Mann and Kesten, *Heart of Europe.*

Die Monduhr, 1933. Eng. tr., "The Moon Watch," in *Story,* X (no. 54, 1937), 86–102.

Politische Novelle, 1928. Eng. tr., *The Persians Are Coming,* New York, Knopf, 1929.

Der Reisepass, 1937. Eng. tr., *Lost Heritage,* New York, Viking Press, 1937. (British ed., *Closed Frontiers.*)

Sechzehntausend Francs, 1940. Eng. tr., "16,000 Francs," in *Decision,* I (nos. 4–6, 1941), 44–52, 22–35, 28–20.

Sturm im Wasserglas, 1930. Eng. tr., *Storm in a Teacup,* London, French, 1937. (Published also under title, *Storm over Patsy.*)

Tage des Königs, 1935. Eng. tr., *The Days of the King,* New York, Readers Club, 1942.

Die Tochter, 1943. Eng. tr., *One Fair Daughter,* New York, Viking Press, 1943.

Trenck, Roman eines Günstlings, 1931. Eng. tr., *Trenck, Love-Story of a Favourite,* New York, Knopf, 1928.

Das Weib auf dem Tiere, 1921. Eng. tr., *Young Madame Conti,* London, French, 1938.

Zwölftausend, 1927. Eng. tr., *Twelve Thousand,* New York, Knopf, 1928.

REFERENCE

Hofe, H. von, "Literature in Exile: Bruno Frank," *German Quarterly,* XVIII (1945), 56–91.

FRANK, LEONHARD

Atmen. Eng. tr., "Breathe," in Mann and Kesten, *Heart of Europe.* (Also in *In the Last Coach and Other Stories,* listed below.)

Bruder und Schwester, 1929. Eng. tr., *Brother and Sister,* London, Davies, 1931.

Der Bürger, 1924. Eng. tr., *Clamoring Self,* New York, Putnam, 1930. (British ed., *A Middle Class Man.*)

Im Letzten Wagen, 1925. Eng. tr., "In the Last Coach," in *In the Last Coach and Other Stories,* London, Lane, 1934.

Karl und Anna, 1927. Eng. tr., *Carl and Anna,* New York, Putnam, 1930.

Das Ochsenfurter Männerquartett, 1927. Eng. tr., *The Singers,* New York, Holt, 1933.

Die Räuberbande, 1914. Eng. tr., *The Robber Band,* London, Davies, 1930.

Die Ursache, 1929. Eng. tr., *The Cause of the Crime,* London, Davies, 1931.

"Der Vater" (from *Der Mensch ist gut,* 1919). Eng. tr., "The Father," in Steinhauer and Jessiman, *Modern German Short Stories.*

Von drei Millionen drei, 1931. Eng. tr., *Three of the Three Million,* London, Lane, 1936.

REFERENCE

Whittaker, E., "Leonhard Frank," *Bookman* (London), LXXXI (1931), 108–109.

FREUD, SIGMUND

Basic Writings, New York, Modern Library, 1938.

Civilization, War, and Death: Selections, London, Hogarth Press, 1939. (Contains on pp. 98–102 a list of translations into English of Freud's works up to July, 1937.)

Collected Papers, New York, International Psycho-Analytical Press, 1924–25. 4 vols.

The Living Thoughts of Freud. New York, Longmans, Green, 1941.

REFERENCES

Bartlett, F. H., *Sigmund Freud,* London, Gollancz, 1938.

Freud, S., *Autobiography,* New York, Norton, 1935.

Hoffmann, F. J., *Freudianism and the Literary Mind,* Baton Rouge, Louisiana State Univ. Press, 1945.

Mann, T., *Freud, Goethe, Wagner,* New York, Knopf, 1937.

FREYTAG, GUSTAV

(For translations see Morgan's *Critical Bibliography,* pp. 126–127.)

REFERENCE

Silz, W., "Freytag's 'Soll und Haben' and Raabe's 'Der Hungerpastor,' " *Modern Language Notes,* XXXIX (1924), 10–17.

GEORGE, STEFAN

More Poems, tr. C. F. McIntyre, Norfolk, Conn., New Directions, 1945.

Poems, tr. C. N. Valhope and E. Morwitz, New York, Pantheon Books, 1943.

Translations from the German of Stefan George by C. Scott, London, Mathews, 1910. (Vigo Cabinet Series, no. 71.)

SELECTIONS

Broicher, *German Lyrists of Today.*

Deutsch and Yarmolinsky, *Contemporary German Poetry.*
Francke, *German Classics,* Vol. XVIII.
Münsterberg, *Harvest of German Verse.*
Van Doren, *Anthology of World Poetry.*

REFERENCES

Bentley, E. R., *A Century of Hero-Worship,* Philadelphia, Lippincott, 1944, pp. 214–230.

Bowra, C. M., *The Heritage of Symbolism,* London, Macmillan, 1943, pp. 98–143.

Burkhard, A., "Stefan George, 1868–1933," *German Quarterly,* VII (1934), 49–57.

Butler, *The Tyranny of Greece over Germany,* pp. 322–331.

Closs, *Genius of the German Lyric,* pp. 424–436.

Henel, H., "Stefan George," *Queen's Quarterly,* XLIV (1937), 533–541.

Kahler, E., *Man the Measure,* New York, Pantheon Books, 1943, pp. 584–587.

Morwitz, E., "Stefan George," in George, Stefan, *Poems* (listed above), pp. 9–36.

Raybould, A. N., "Stefan George and the Germany of To-day," *Contemporary Review,* CXLVII (1935), 729–734.

Sommerfeld, M., in *George, Hofmannsthal, Rilke,* New York, Norton, 1938.

Stark, T., "Stefan George and the Reform of the German Lyric," *Modern Language Notes,* XXXIV (1919), 1–7.

Stirk, S. D., "Stefan George and the 'New Empire,' " *German Life and Letters,* II (1938), 175–187.

Zabel, M. D., "Stefan George," *Poetry,* XLIII (1934), 333–338.

GLAESER, ERNST

Jahrgang 1902, 1928. Eng. tr., *Class of 1902,* New York, Viking Press, 1929.

Der letzte Zivilist, 1935. Eng. tr., *The Last Civilian,* New York, McBride, 1935.

Der Staat ohne Arbeitslose, 1931 (with F. K. Weiskopf). Eng. tr., *Land Without Unemployment,* London, Lawrence, 1932.

Das Unvergängliche, 1936. Chapter III tr. as "The Cherry Feast," in Maugham, W. S., ed., *Tellers of Tales,* New York, Doubleday, Doran, 1939.

GRAF, OSKAR MARIA

Bolwieser, 1931. Eng. tr., *Station Master,* London, Chatto & Windus, 1933.

Einer gegen alle, 1932. Eng. tr., *The Wolf,* London, Dickson, 1934.

Life of My Mother, New York, Howell, Soskin, 1940.

Wir sind Gefangene, 1927. Eng. tr., *Prisoners All,* New York, O. M. Graf, 1943.

SELECTIONS

Twice-a-Year, no. 5–6 (1940–41), 215–221.

GRAFF, SIGMUND, and CARL HINTZE

Die endlose Strasse, 1929. Eng. tr., *The Endless Road,* London, Allen & Unwin, 1930.

GRIESE, FRIEDRICH

Der Saatgang, 1932. Eng. tr., "The Sower," in Steinhauer and Jessiman, *Modern German Short Stories.*

Winter, 1927. Eng. tr., *Winter,* New York, Longmans, Green, 1929.

REFERENCE

Hodsoll, E. R., "German Literature To-day," *Contemporary Review,* CLV (1939), 709–716.

GRIMM, HANS

Englisch-deutsche Probleme im Wandel unserer Zeit, 1937. Eng. tr., "Contemporary Anglo-German Problems," in *German Life and Letters,* II (1937–38), 1–13.

Englische Rede; wie ich den Engländer sehe, Gütersloh, Bertelsmann, 1938. (German and English text.)

REFERENCES

Danton, G. H., "Hans Grimm's 'Volk ohne Raum,'" *Monatshefte für deutschen Unterricht,* XXVII (1935), 33–43.

Frey, J. R., "The Function of the Writer," *Monatshefte für deutschen Unterricht,* XXXII (1940), 266–278.

House, R. T., "The South African Stories of Hans Grimm," *American-German Review*, VI (1939), 16–17, 37.

GUNDOLF, FRIEDRICH

Caesar, Geschichte seines Ruhms, 1924. Eng. tr., *Mantle of Caesar*, New York, Vanguard Press, 1928.

HAECKER, THEODOR

Søren Kierkegaard, 1913. Eng. tr., same title, London, Oxford Univ. Press, 1937.

Vergil, Vater des Abendlandes, 1931. Eng. tr., *Virgil, Father of the West*, London, Sheed & Ward, 1934.

HANDEL-MAZZETTI, ENRICA von

Jesse und Maria, 1906. Eng. tr., *Jesse and Maria*, New York, Holt, 1931.

HARTMANN, EDUARD von

Philosophie des Unbewussten, 1869. Eng. tr., *Philosophy of the Unconscious*, London, Paul, Trench, Trubner, 1931.

(Other works have been translated.)

HASENCLEVER, WALTER

Napoleon greift ein, 1929. Excerpt tr. as "Napoleon and Landru, an Imaginary Conversation," in *Living Age*, CCCXXXVII (1929), 433–440.

REFERENCES

Boyd, E. A., *Studies from Ten Literatures*, New York, Scribner's, 1925, pp. 231–250.

Chandler, F. W., *Modern Continental Playwrights*, New York, Harper, 1931, pp. 366–382.

HAUPTMANN, CARL

Aus dem grossen Kriege, 1915. Eng. tr., "The Dead are Singing," in *Texas Review*, I (1916), 250–256.

Ephraims Breite, 1900. Eng. tr., same title, in *Poet Lore*, XII (1900), 465–536.

Krieg, ein Tedeum, 1914. Eng. tr., "War, a Tedeum," in *Drama*, VI (1916), 597–653.

REFERENCE

Ende, A. von, "Carl Hauptmann," *Drama,* VI (1916), 582–596.

HAUPTMANN, GERHART

Atlantis, 1912. Eng. tr., same title, New York, Huebsch, 1912.

Buch der Leidenschaft, 1930. Eng. tr., *Book of Passion,* London, 1930.

Die Insel der grossen Mutter, 1925. Eng. tr., *The Island of the Great Mother,* New York, Huebsch, 1925.

Der Ketzer von Soana, 1918. Eng. tr., *The Heretic of Soana,* New York, Modern Library, 1928.

Der Narr in Christo Emanuel Quint, 1910. Eng. tr., *The Fool in Christ, Emanuel Quint,* New York, Huebsch, 1926.

Parsival, 1914. Eng. tr., *Parsival,* New York, Macmillan, 1915.

Phantom, 1922. Eng. tr., *The Phantom,* New York, Huebsch, 1922.

COLLECTION

Dramatic Works, ed. L. Lewisohn, New York, Huebsch (continued by Viking Press), 1912–29, 9 vols.

Contents—Vol. I: Before Dawn; The Weavers; The Beaver Coat; The Conflagration. Vol. II: Drayman Henschel; Rose Bernd; The Rats. Vol. III: The Reconciliation; Lonely Lives; Colleague Crampton; Michael Kramer. Vol. IV: The Assumption of Hannele; The Sunken Bell; Henry of Auë. Vol. V: Schluck and Jau; And Pippa Dances; Charlemagne's Hostage. Vol. VI: The Maidens of the Mount; Griselda; Gabriel Schilling's Flight. Vol. VII: Commemoration Masque; The Bow of Odysseus; Elga; Helios; Pastoral. Vol. VIII: Indipohdi; The White Saviour; A Winter Ballad. Vol. IX: Florian Geyer; Veland.

REFERENCES

Buck, P. M., *Directions in Contemporary Literature,* New York, Oxford Univ. Press, 1942, pp. 37–57.

Campbell, T. M., "Gerhart Hauptmann, Christian or Pagan," *Modern Language Journal,* VIII (1924), 353–361.

Closs, A., "Gerhart Hauptmann," *Contemporary Review,* CXLII (1932), 729–735.

Dukes, A., *Modern Dramatists*, London, Palmer, 1911, pp. 78–95.

Heuser, F. W. J., "Early Influences on the Intellectual Development of G. Hauptmann," *Germanic Review*, V (1930), 38–57.

——, "Gerhart Hauptmann and Frank Wedekind," *Germanic Review*, XX (1945), 54–68.

——, "Hauptmann's 'Die Tochter der Kathedrale,'" *Germanic Review*, XV (1940), 137–145.

——, "Hauptmann's 'Germanen und Römer,'" *Germanic Review*, XVII (1942), 174–196.

——, "The Mystical Hauptmann," *Germanic Review*, VII (1932), 32–44.

Klenze, *From Goethe to Hauptmann*, pp. 223–275.

Lessing, *Masters in Modern German Literature*, pp. 87–134.

Lewisohn, L., *Modern Drama*, New York, Huebsch, 1915, pp. 110–128.

——, *Cities and Men*, New York, Harper, 1927, pp. 121–132.

Mann, T., "To Gerhart Hauptmann," *Living Age*, CCCXLIV (1933), 60–65.

Randall, A. W. G., "Gerhart Hauptmann," *Contemporary Review*, CXXII (1922), 636–644.

Reichart, W. A., "Fifty Years of Hauptmann Study in America (1894–1944): A Bibliography," *Monatshefte für deutschen Unterricht*, XXXVII (1945), 1–31.

——, "Iphigenie in Delphi," *Germanic Review*, XVII (1942), 221–237.

——, "A Modern German 'Hamlet,'" *Journal of English and Germanic Philology*, XXXI (1932), 27–50.

Wahr, F. B., "Theory and Composition of the Hauptmann Drama," *Germanic Review*, XVII (1942), 163–173.

HAUSER, HEINRICH

Battle Against Time, New York, Scribner's, 1939.

Brackwasser, 1928. Eng. tr., *Bitter Waters*, New York, Liveright, 1929.

Donner überm Meer, 1929. Eng. tr., *Thunder Above the Sea*, New York, Liveright, 1931.

Hitler versus Germany, London, Jarrolds, 1940.

Kampf, 1934. Eng. tr., *Once Your Enemy,* London, Methuen, 1936.

Die letzten Segelschiffe, 1930. Eng. tr., *Fair Winds and Foul,* New York, Liveright, 1932.

Notre Dame von den Wogen, 1937. Eng. tr., *Last Port of Call,* New York, Stackpole, 1938. (Excerpt tr. as *The Folding Father,* Boston, Lothrop, Lee & Shepard, 1942.)

Time Was; Death of a Junker, New York, Reynal & Hitchcock, 1942.

HEIDEGGER, MARTIN

REFERENCES

Bourke, J., "Characteristics of Contemporary German Philosophy," *German Life and Letters,* II (1937–38), 275–289.

Werkmeister, W. H., "An Introduction to Heidegger's 'Existential Philosophy,'" *Philosophy and Phenomenological Research,* II (1941), 79–87.

HEISELER, HENRY von

REFERENCE

Von Gronicka, A., *Henry von Heiseler, a Russo-German Writer,* New York, King's Crown Press, 1944.

HERRMANN-NEISSE, MAX

SELECTIONS

Deutsch and Yarmolinsky, *Contemporary German Poetry.*

HESSE, HERMANN

Blick ins Chaos, 1915. Eng. tr., *In Sight of Chaos,* London, Zwemmer, 1923.

Demian, 1919. Eng. tr., same title, New York, Boni & Liveright, 1923.

Gertrud, 1910. Eng. tr., *Gertrude and I,* New York, International Monthly, 1915.

In der alten Sonne, 1914. Eng. tr., "In the Old Sun," in Francke, *German Classics,* Vol. XIX.

Jakob Boehmes Berufung, 1922. Eng. tr., "Jacob Boehme's Calling," in Mann and Kesten, *Heart of Europe.*

"Notes on the Theme: Imaginative Writing and Criticism," in *This Quarter* (Paris), IV (1931–32), 20–34.

Narziss und Goldmund, 1930. Eng. tr., *Death and the Lover,* New York, Dodd, Mead, 1932.

Der Steppenwolf, 1927. Eng. tr., *Steppenwolf,* New York, Holt, 1929.

SELECTIONS

Deutsch and Yarmolinsky, *Contemporary German Poetry.*

Francke, *German Classics,* Vol. XVIII.

Münsterberg, *Harvest of German Verse.*

Peters, E. C., *Between Two Worlds,* Billericay, Essex, Grey Walls Press, 1941.

Van Doren, *Anthology of World Poetry.*

HEYM, GEORG

SELECTIONS

Deutsch and Yarmolinsky, *Contemporary German Poetry.*

HEYSE, PAUL

(For translations see Morgan's *Critical Bibliography,* pp. 232–234.)

REFERENCES

Brandes, G. M. C., *Creative Spirits of the Nineteenth Century,* New York, Crowell, 1923, pp. 54–105.

Joubert, M., "Paul Heyse," *Contemporary Review,* CXXXVII (1930), 602–608.

HOFMANNSTHAL, HUGO von

Der Abenteurer und die Sängerin, 1899. Excerpt tr. as "The Adventurer and the Singer," in *Warner's Library of the World's Best Literature,* univ. ed., 1917–18, Vol. VIII.

Die ägyptische Helena, 1928. Eng. libretto, *Helen in Egypt,* Berlin, Fürstner, 1928.

Andreas, 1932. Eng. tr., *Andreas, or The United,* London, Dent, 1936.

Ariadne auf Naxos, 1912. Eng. libretto, *Ariadne on Naxos,* Berlin, Fürstner, 1924.

Brief des Lord Chandos, 1901. Eng. tr., "The Letter," in *Rocky Mountain Review,* VI (1942), 1, 3, 11–13.

Buch der Freunde, 1922. Excerpt tr. as "From the Book of Friends," in *Dial,* LXXIII (1922), 23–24.

Cristinas Heimreise, 1910. Eng. tr., *Cristina's Journey Home,* Boston, Badger, 1916. (Also in *Poet Lore,* XXVIII [1917], 129–186.)

Der Dichter und diese Zeit, 1907. Excerpts tr. in Lewisohn, L., *Modern Book of Criticism,* New York, Boni & Liveright, 1919.

Elektra, 1903. Eng. tr., "Electra," in Dickinson, T. H., ed., *Chief Contemporary Dramatists,* 3d ser., Boston, Houghton Mifflin, 1930.

Die Frau im Fenster, 1897. Eng. tr., *Madonna Dianora,* Boston, Badger, 1916. (Also in Shay, Frank, ed., *Fifty Contemporary One-Act Plays,* Cincinnati, Stewart & Kidd, 1920.)

Das gerettete Venedig, 1905. Eng. tr., *Venice Preserved,* Boston, Badger, 1915. (Also in *Poet Lore,* XXVI [1915], 529–643.)

Die Hochzeit der Sobeide, 1899. Eng. tr., "The Marriage of Sobeide," in Francke, *German Classics,* Vol. XX.

Jedermann, 1911. Eng. tr., *The Play of Everyman,* San Francisco, Robertson, 1917.

Josephslegende, 1914. Eng. libretto, *The Legend of Joseph,* Berlin, Fürstner, 1914.

Lucidor, 1919. Eng. tr., same title, in *Dial,* LXXIII (1922), 121–132.

Reitergeschichte, 1899. Eng. tr., "Cavalry Patrol," in Maugham, W. S., ed., *Tellers of Tales,* New York, Doubleday, Doran, 1939. (Also in Mann and Kesten, *Heart of Europe.*)

Der Rosenkavalier, 1911. Eng. libretto, *The Rose Bearer,* Berlin, Fürstner, 1914.

Der Tod des Tizian, 1892. Eng. tr., *Death of Titian,* Boston, Four Seas Co., 1920. (Also in Francke, *German Classics,* Vol. XVII.)

Der Tor und der Tod, 1893. Eng. tr., *Death and the Fool,* Boston, Badger, 1913. (Also in *Poet Lore,* XXIV [1913], 253–267;

ibid. [a new translation], XLV [1939], 5–21; Francke, *German Classics*, Vol. XVII; Moses, M. J., *Representative One-Act Plays by Continental Authors*, Boston, Little, Brown, 1926; *Colorado College Publications*, Gen. ser., no. 172 [1930].)

Der weisse Fächer, 1897. Eng. tr. of first part, "The White Fan," in *Mask*, I (1908–09), 232–234.

SELECTIONS

Bithell, *Contemporary German Poetry.*

Broicher, *German Lyrists of Today.*

Francke, *German Classics*, Vol. XVII.

Harvard Advocate, CXXVIII (1942), 24.

Lyrical Poems, tr. C. W. Stork, New Haven, Yale Univ. Press, 1918.

REFERENCES

Dukes, A., *Modern Dramatists*, London, Palmer, 1911, pp. 159–180.

Gilbert, M. E., "Hugo von Hofmannsthal and England," *German Life and Letters*, I (1937), 182–193.

Gilbert, M. E., in Hofmannsthal, H. von, *Der Tor und der Tod*, Oxford, Blackwell, 1943.

Gross, F., "Hugo von Hofmannsthal," *Contemporary Review*, CXLIX (1936), 709–714.

Hewett-Thayer, H. W., "Introduction to 'The Fool and Death,'" *Colorado College Publications*, Gen. ser., no. 172 (1930).

Joubert, M., "H. v. Hofmannsthal and his Collaboration with Richard Strauss," *Contemporary Review*, CXXXVI (1929), 632–637.

Karlweis, M., "Hugo von Hofmannsthal," *Criterion*, XIII (no. 50, 1933), 25–50.

Sommerfeld, M., in *George, Hofmannsthal, Rilke*, New York, Norton, 1938.

Stork, C. W., "Hofmannsthal as a Lyric Poet," in Hofmannsthal, H. von, *Lyrical Poems* (listed above).

Walter, E., "Hugo von Hofmannsthal, an Exponent of Modern Lyricism," *Colonnade*, XII (1916), 111–122.

Wood, F., "Hofmannsthal's Aesthetics; a Survey Based on His Prose Works," *PMLA*, LV (1940), 253–265.

HOLZ, ARNO

SELECTIONS

Bithell, *Contemporary German Poetry.*

Deutsch and Yarmolinsky, *Contemporary German Poetry.*

Poet Lore, XXXIV (1923), 154–156.

Transition, no. 2 (1927), 145–148.

Van Doren, *Anthology of World Poetry.*

REFERENCES

Closs, *Genius of the German Lyric,* pp. 384–397.

——, "New Forms in the German Lyric," *Poetry Review,* XXI (1930), 99–110.

Lessing, *Masters in Modern German Literature,* pp. 135–165.

HUCH, RICARDA

Erinnerungen von Ludolf Ursleu dem Jüngeren, 1893. Eng. tr., *Eros Invincible,* New York, Macaulay, 1931.

Der Fall Deruga, 1917. Eng. tr., *The Deruga Trial,* New York, Macaulay, 1929.

Die Geschichten von Garibaldi, 1906. Eng. tr., *Garibaldi and the New Italy,* New York, Knopf, 1928–29, 2 vols.

Das Judengrab, 1905. Eng. tr., "The Jew's Grave," in Steinhauer and Jessiman, *Modern German Short Stories.*

"Romantische Ehe" (from Keyserling, H. von, *Das Ehe-Buch,* 1925). Eng. tr., "Romantic Marriage," in Keyserling, H. von, *Book of Marriage,* New York, Harcourt, Brace, 1926.

SELECTIONS

Bithell, *Contemporary German Poetry.*

Francke, *German Classics,* Vol. XVIII.

REFERENCE

Hewett-Thayer, *Modern German Novel,* pp. 103–130.

HUSSERL, EDMUND

REFERENCES

Farber, M., *The Foundation of Phenomenology; Edmund Husserl and the Quest for a Rigorous Science of Philosophy,* Cambridge, [Mass.], Harvard Univ. Press, 1943.

Philosophical Essays in Memory of Edmund Husserl, Cambridge, [Mass.], Harvard Univ. Press, 1940.

Welch, E. P., *The Philosophy of Edmund Husserl,* New York, Columbia Univ. Press, 1941.

JASPERS, KARL

Die geistige Situation der Zeit, 1931. Eng. tr., *Man in the Modern Age,* London, Routledge, 1933.

REFERENCE

Bourke, J., "Characteristics of Contemporary German Philosophy," *German Life and Letters,* II (1937–38), 275–289.

JÜNGER, ERNST

In Stahlgewittern, 1920. Eng. tr., *Storm of Steel,* Garden City, N.Y., Doubleday, Doran, 1929.

Das Wäldchen 125, 1925. Eng. tr., *Copse 125; a Chronicle from the Trench Warfare of 1918,* London, Chatto & Windus, 1930.

REFERENCES

Guerster-Steinhausen, E., "The Prophet of German Nihilism—Ernst Juenger," *Review of Politics,* VII (1945), 199–209.

Kahler, E., *Man the Measure,* New York, Pantheon Books, 1943, pp. 593–597.

Pfeiler, *War and the German Mind,* pp. 109–116.

Stirk, *The Prussian Spirit,* pp. 91–96.

JUNG, CARL GUSTAV

Psychologische Typen, 1921. Eng. tr., *Psychological Types,* New York, Harcourt, Brace, 1923.

Seelenprobleme der Gegenwart, 1931. Eng. tr., with some material added, *Modern Man in Search of a Soul,* London, Paul, Trench, Trübner, 1933.

(Other works have been translated.)

REFERENCES

Jacobi, J., *Psychology of Jung,* New Haven, Yale Univ. Press, 1943.

——, "An Interview with C. G. Jung," *Horizon,* VIII (1943), 372–381.

KÄSTNER, ERICH

Drei Männer im Schnee, 1934. Eng. tr., *Three Men in the Snow,* London, Cape, 1935.

Emil und die Detektive, 1929. Eng. tr., *Emil and the Detectives,* New York, Doubleday, Doran, 1930.

Emil und die drei Zwillinge, 1935. Eng. tr., *Emil and the Three Twins,* London, Cape, 1935.

Fabian, 1931. Eng. tr., same title, New York, Dodd, Mead, 1932.

Das fliegende Klassenzimmer, 1933. Eng. tr., *The Flying Classroom,* London, Cape, 1934.

Der 35. Mai oder Konrad reitet in die Südsee, 1932. Eng. tr., *The 35th of May; or, Conrad's Ride to the South Seas,* New York, Dodd, Mead, 1934.

Pünktchen und Anton, 1931. Eng. tr., *Annaluise and Anton,* New York, Dodd, Mead, 1933.

Die verschwundene Miniatur, 1936. Eng. tr., *The Missing Miniature,* New York, American Mercury, 1939.

REFERENCE

Hofrichter, R. J., "Erich Kästner as a Representative of 'Neue Sachlichkeit,' " *German Quarterly,* V (1932), 173–177.

KAFKA, FRANZ

Amerika, 1927. Eng. tr., *America,* Norfolk, Conn., New Directions, 1940.

Beim Bau der chinesischen Mauer, 1931. Eng. tr., *The Great Wall of China and Other Pieces,* London, Secker, 1933.

"Der Geier" (from *Gesammelte Schriften,* Vol. V, 1936). Eng. tr., "The Vulture," in *Twice-a-Year,* no. 1 (1938), 131.

Ein Hungerkünstler, 1923. Individual stories tr.: "Erstes Leid." Eng. tr., "First Grief," in *Life and Letters To-day,* XVI (1937), 57–59. "Eine kleine Frau." Eng. tr., "A Little Woman," in *Accent,* III (1943), 223–227. "Ein Hungerkünstler." Eng. tr., "The Hunger-Artist," in Steinhauer and Jessiman, *Modern German Short Stories.* "Josefine die Sängerin." Eng. tr., "Josephine the Songstress," in *Partisan Review,* IX (1942), 213–228.

In der Strafkolonie, 1919. Eng. tr., "In the Penal Colony," in *Partisan Review,* VIII (1941), 98–107.

Ein Landarzt, 1919. Individual stories tr.: "Ein Landarzt." Eng. tr., "A Country Doctor," in *New Directions in Prose and Poetry, 1940,* Norfolk, Conn., New Directions, 1940. "Vor dem Gesetz." Eng. tr., "Before the Law," in *New Directions in Prose and Poetry, 1941,* Norfolk, Conn., New Directions, 1941. "Schakale und Araber." Eng. tr., "Jackals and Arabs," in *New Directions, 1942,* Norfolk, Conn., New Directions, 1942. "Die Sorge des Hausvaters." Eng. tr., "The Housefather's Care," in *Transition,* no. 27 (1938), 160–161.

"Prometheus" (from *Gesammelte Schriften,* Vol. V, 1936). Eng. tr., "A Fragment," in *Transition,* no. 23 (1935), 25.

Der Prozess, 1925. Eng. tr., *The Trial,* New York, Knopf, 1937.

Das Schloss, 1926. Eng. tr., *The Castle,* New York, Knopf, 1941.

Das Urteil, 1913. Eng. tr., "Sentence," in Jolas, E., ed., *Transition Stories,* New York, McFee, 1929.

Die Verwandlung, 1916. Eng. tr., *The Metamorphosis,* London, Parton Press, 1937.

SELECTIONS

A Franz Kafka Miscellany, New York, Twice-a-Year Press, 1940.

REFERENCES

Arendt, H., "Franz Kafka," *Partisan Review,* XI (1944), 412–422.

Belgion, M., "Kafka," *Criterion,* XVIII (1938), 13–28.

Brod, M., "Franz Kafka's Letter to His Father," *Transition,* no. 27 (1938), 295–313.

Hoffmann, F. J., *Freudianism and the Literary Mind,* Baton Rouge, Louisiana State Univ. Press, 1945, pp. 181–229.

A Franz Kafka Miscellany (listed above).

Kelly, J., "Franz Kafka's 'Trial' and the Theology of Crisis," *Southern Review,* V (1939–40), 748–766.

Muir, E., "A Note on Franz Kafka," *Bookman* (New York), LXXII (1930–31), 235–241.

Rahv, P., "The Hero as a Lonely Man," *Kenyon Review,* I (1939), 60–74.

Slochower, *No Voice Is Wholly Lost,* pp. 103–125.

Thomas, R. H., "Franz Kafka and the Religious Aspects of Expressionism," *German Life and Letters,* II (1938), 42–49.

Warren, A., "Kosmos Kafka," *Southern Review,* VII (1941–42), 350–365.

Wolff, K., "Franz Kafka," *Twice-a-Year,* no. 8–9 (1942), 273–279.

KAISER, GEORG

Der Brand im Opernhaus, 1919. Eng. tr., "Fire in the Opera House," in Katzin, W., comp., *Eight European Plays,* New York, Brentano's, 1927.

Gas, 1918, 1920. Eng. tr., "Gas, I and II," in Tucker, S. M., ed., *Modern Continental Plays,* New York, Harper, 1929. (*Gas I* also pub. Boston, Small, Maynard, 1924.)

Die Koralle, 1917. Eng. tr., "Coral," in Tucker, S. M., ed., *Modern Continental Plays,* New York, Harper, 1929.

Oktobertag, 1928. Eng. tr., *Phantom Lover,* New York, Brentano's, 1928.

Villa Aurea, 1940. Eng. tr., *Vera,* New York, Alliance Book Corp., 1939. (British ed., *A Villa in Sicily.*)

Von Morgens bis Mitternacht, 1916. Eng. tr., "From Morn to Midnight," in *Poet Lore,* XXXI (1920), 317–363. (Also in Dickinson, T. H., ed., *Chief Contemporary Dramatists,* 3d ser., Boston, Houghton Mifflin, 1930; and Moses, M. J., *Dramas of Modernism,* Boston, Little, Brown, 1941.)

REFERENCES

Chandler, F. W., *Modern Continental Playwrights,* New York, Harper, 1931, pp. 407–437.

Drake, W. A., *Contemporary European Writers,* New York, Day, 1928, pp. 87–97.

Koenigsgarten, H. F., "The Leading Playwright of Expressionism," *German Life and Letters,* III (1939), 195–205.

KANTOROWICZ, ERNST

Kaiser Friedrich II, 1927. Eng. tr., *Frederick II,* New York, R. R. Smith, 1931.

KELLER, GOTTFRIED

Der grüne Heinrich, 1854–55. Excerpt tr. as "Little Meret, Green-Coat Henry's Story," in *Poet Lore,* XVII (1906), 50–58.

(For other translations see Morgan's *Critical Bibliography,* pp. 263–264, 726.)

REFERENCES

Fairley, B., in Keller, G., *Der grüne Heinrich,* New York, Oxford Univ. Press, 1926.

Furst, N., "The Structure of 'L'Education Sentimentale' and 'Der grüne Heinrich,' " *PMLA,* LVI (1941), 249–260.

Hauch, E. F., *Gottfried Keller as a Democratic Idealist,* New York, Columbia Univ. Press, 1916.

Hay, M., *The Story of a Swiss Poet: a Study of Gottfried Keller's Life and Works,* Berne, Wyss, 1920.

Klenze, *From Goethe to Hauptmann; Studies in a Changing Culture,* pp. 105–130.

Kramer, P. M., *The Cyclical Method of Composition in G. Keller's Sinngedicht,* New York, New York University, 1939.

Randall, A. W. G., "Gottfried Keller," *Contemporary Review,* CXVI (1919), 532–537.

Robertson, J. G., *Essays and Addresses on Literature,* London, Routledge, 1935.

KESTEN, HERMANN

Copernicus and His World, New York, Roy, 1945.

Ferdinand und Isabella, 1936. Eng. tr., *Spanish Fire,* London, Hutchinson, 1937.

Glückliche Menschen, 1931. Eng. tr., *Happy Man!* London, Lane, 1935.

Joseph sucht die Freiheit, 1927. Eng. tr., *Joseph Breaks Free,* London, Constable, 1930.

Die Kinder von Gernika, 1939. Eng. tr., *Children of Guernica,* New York, Longmans, Green, 1939.

König Philipp der Zweite, 1938. Eng. tr., *I, the King,* New York, Alliance Book Corp., 1940.

Oberst Kock, 1942. Eng. tr., "Colonel Kock," in Mann and Kesten, *Heart of Europe.*

KEYSERLING, EDUARD von

(For translations see Morgan's *Critical Bibliography,* pp. 265, 727.)

REFERENCE

Hewitt, T. B., "The Novels of Eduard von Keyserling," *German Quarterly,* IV (1931), 51–55.

KEYSERLING, HERMANN A. von

Amerika, der Aufgang einer neuen Welt, 1931. Eng. tr., *America Set Free,* New York, Harper, 1929.

Das Reisetagebuch eines Philosophen, 1919. Eng. tr., *Travel Diary of a Philosopher,* London, Cape, 1925.

Das Spektrum Europas, 1928. Eng. tr., *Europe,* New York, Harcourt, Brace, 1928.

(Other works have been translated.)

REFERENCE

Parks, M. G., *Introduction to Keyserling; an Account of the Man and His Work,* London, Cape, 1934.

KLABUND (i.e., Alfred Henschke)

Bracke, ein Eulenspiegel-Roman, 1918. Eng. tr., *Brackie the Fool,* New York, Putnam's, 1927.

Borgia, Roman einer Familie, 1928. Eng. tr., *The Incredible Borgias,* New York, Liveright, 1929.

Der Kreidekreis, 1925. Eng. tr., *The Circle of Chalk,* London, Heinemann, 1929.

Pjotr, Roman eines Zaren, 1923. Eng. tr., *Peter the Czar,* New York, Putnam's, 1925.

REFERENCES

Paulsen, W., "Klabund," *German Life and Letters,* III (1938–39), 222–230.

Scheffauer, E. T., "Some German Post-War Lyric Poets," *Poetry Review,* XXVIII (1937), 205–221.

KLAGES, LUDWIG

Die Grundlagen der Charakterkunde, 1928. Eng. tr., *Science of Character,* London, Allen & Unwin, 1929.

(Other works have been translated.)

REFERENCE

Baer, L., "The Literary Criticism of Ludwig Klages and the Klages School," *Journal of English and Germanic Philology,* XL (1941), 91–138.

KOESTLER, ARTHUR

Arrival and Departure, New York, Macmillan, 1943.

Darkness at Noon, New York, Macmillan, 1941.

Dialogue with Death, New York, Macmillan, 1942.

The Gladiators, New York, Macmillan, 1939.

Scum of the Earth, New York, Macmillan, 1941.

Spanish Testament, London, Gollancz, 1937.

REFERENCE

Davis, R. G., "The Sharp Horns of Koestler's Dilemma," *Antioch Review,* IV (1944–5), 503–517.

KOLBENHEYER, ERWIN GUIDO

Amor Dei, 1908. Eng. tr., *God-intoxicated Man,* London, Nicholson & Watson, 1933.

Meister Joachim Pausewang, 1910. Eng. tr., *A Winter Chronicle,* London, Lane, 1938.

Völkerverständigung, 1935. Eng. tr., *Promotion of Understanding Between the Nations,* Munich, Rotary Club, 1935.

Wie wurde der deutsche Roman Dichtung? 1937. Eng. tr., "Art of the Novel," *German Life and Letters,* I (1936–37), 18–30.

REFERENCES

Frey, J. R., "The Function of the Writer," *Monatshefte für deutschen Unterricht,* XXXII (1940), 266–278.

Reinhardt, K. F., "Kolbenheyer a Metaphysician?" *Germanic Review,* XII (1937), 196–202.

Sepmeier, K. A., "Kolbenheyer's 'Zeitdramen,'" *Monatshefte für deutschen Unterricht,* XXVII (1935), 226–232.

KRAUS, KARL

Poems, Boston, Four Seas, 1930.

KURZ, ISOLDE

Florentiner Novellen, 1890. Eng. tr., *Tales of Florence,* London, Melrose, 1919.

SELECTIONS

Francke, *German Classics,* Vol. XVIII.

Münsterberg, *Harvest of German Verse.*

LAMPEL, PETER MARTIN

Verratene Jungen, 1929. Eng. tr., *Youth Betrayed,* London, Shaylor, 1930.

LAMPRECHT, KARL

Moderne Geschichtswissenschaft, 1905. Eng. tr., *What Is History?* New York, Macmillan, 1905.

LASKER-SCHÜLER, ELSE

SELECTIONS

Bithell, *Contemporary German Poetry.*

Deutsch and Yarmolinsky, *Contemporary German Poetry.*

Transition, no. 1 (1927), 123; no. 5 (1927), 122.

LE FORT, GERTRUD von

Die ewige Frau, Die Frau in der Zeit, Die zeitlose Frau, 1934. Excerpt tr. as "Woman in Time," in *Commonweal,* XXIII (1936), 513–515.

Hymnen an die Kirche, 1924. Eng. tr., *Hymns to the Church,* New York, Sheed & Ward, 1938.

Die Letzte am Schafott, 1931. Eng. tr., *Song of the Scaffold,* New York, Holt, 1933.

Der Papst aus dem Ghetto, 1930. Eng. tr., *The Pope from the Ghetto,* New York, Sheed & Ward, 1934.

Das Schweisstuch der Veronica, 1928. Eng. tr., *The Veil of Veronica,* New York, Sheed & Ward, 1932.

REFERENCE

Danton, G. H., "Gertrud von Le Fort," *Books Abroad*, XIII (1939), 283–288.

LERSCH, HEINRICH

REFERENCE

Hodsoll, E. R., "German Literature To-day," *Contemporary Review*, CLV (1939), 709–716.

LILIENCRON, DETLEV von

SELECTIONS

Bithell, *Contemporary German Poetry.*

Coxwell, C. F., *German Poetry*, London, Daniel, 1938.

Deutsch and Yarmolinsky, *Contemporary German Poetry.*

Francke, *German Classics*, Vol. XVIII.

Van Doren, *Anthology of World Poetry.*

REFERENCES

Burkhard, A., "The Language of Detlev von Liliencron's Lyrics and Ballads," *Journal of English and Germanic Philology*, XXX (1931), 236–254.

——, "Progress in Poetry," *Journal of English and Germanic Philology*, XXXI (1932), 173–199.

Lessing, *Masters in Modern German Literature*, pp. 35–62.

Schumann, D. W., "Detlev von Liliencron," *Monatshefte für deutschen Unterricht*, XXXVI (1944), 385–408; XXXVII (1945), 65–87.

MACH, ERNST

Die Analyse der Empfindungen und das Verhältniss des Physischen zum Psychischen, 1886. Eng. tr., *The Analysis of Sensations*, Chicago, Open Court Pub. Co., 1914.

MANN, HEINRICH

Das Bekenntnis zum Übernationalen, 1933. Eng. tr., "The Supernational Manifesto," in Mann and Kesten, *Heart of Europe.*

Der blaue Engel, 1930. Eng. tr., *Blue Angel*, London, Jarrolds, 1932. (Film version of *Professor Unrat.*)

Ein ernstes Leben, 1932. Eng. tr., *Hill of Lies,* New York, Dutton, 1935.

Eugénie oder die Bürgerzeit, 1928. Eng. tr., *Royal Woman,* New York, Macaulay, 1930.

"The German European," *Decision,* II (no. 4, 1941), 36–39.

Die Göttinnen, 1903. Eng. tr. of Vol. I, *Diana,* New York, Coward-McCann, 1929.

Im Schlaraffenland, 1900. Eng. tr., *In the Land of Cockaigne,* New York, Macaulay, 1929. (British ed., *Berlin, the Land of Cockaigne.*)

Die Jugend des Königs Henri Quatre, 1935. Eng. tr., *Young Henry of Navarre,* New York, Knopf, 1937. (British ed., *King Wren: the Youth of Henri IV.*)

"Jungfrauen" (from *Stürmische Morgen,* 1907). Eng. tr., "Virgins," in *Dial,* LXXVI (1924), 123–132.

Die kleine Stadt, 1909. Eng. tr., *The Little Town,* Boston, Houghton Mifflin, 1931.

The Living Thoughts of Nietzsche Presented by Heinrich Mann, New York, Longmans, Green, 1939.

Madame Legros, 1913. Eng. tr., same title, in Katzin, W., comp., *Eight European Plays,* New York, Brentano's, 1927.

Mutter Marie, 1927. Eng. tr., *Mother Mary,* New York, Simon & Schuster, 1928.

"Pippo Spano" (from *Flöten und Dolche,* 1904–05). Eng. tr., same title, in Maugham, W. S., ed., *Tellers of Tales,* New York, Doubleday, Doran, 1939.

Professor Unrat, 1905. Eng. tr., *Small Town Tyrant,* New York, Creative Age Press, 1944.

Der Untertan, 1918. Eng. tr., *The Patrioteer,* New York, Harcourt, Brace, 1921.

Die Vollendung des Königs Henri Quatre, 1938. Eng. tr., *Henry, King of France,* New York, Knopf, 1939. (British ed., *Henri Quatre.*)

REFERENCES

Gross, F., "Heinrich Mann," *Contemp. Rev.,* CLX (1941), 120–123.

Hofe, H. von, "German Literature in Exile: Heinrich Mann," *German Quarterly*, XVII (1944), 88–92.

Kayser, R., "Heinrich Mann," *Books Abroad*, XV (1941), 401–405.

Motyleva, J., "Heinrich Mann," *International Literature* (Moscow), 1937, no. 9, 17–32.

Slochower, *No Voice Is Wholly Lost*, pp. 282–285.

MANN, KLAUS

Alexander, Roman der Utopie, 1929. Eng. tr., *Alexander*, New York, Brewer & Warren, 1930.

André Gide, New York, Creative Age Press, 1943.

Escape to Life (with Erika Mann), Boston, Houghton Mifflin, 1939.

"Europe—America," in *Twice-a-Year*, no. 3–4 (1939–40), 148–149.

Flucht in den Norden, 1934. Eng. tr., *Journey into Freedom*, New York, Knopf, 1936.

Kindernovelle, 1926. Eng. tr., *The Fifth Child*, New York, Boni & Liveright, 1927.

Ludwig Zoffke, 1926. Eng. tr., same title, in Eaton, R., ed., *Best Continental Stories of 1926*, New York, Dodd, Mead, 1927.

The Other Germany (with Erika Mann), New York, Modern Age Books, 1940.

"The Present Greatness of Walt Whitman," *Decision*, I (no. 4, 1941), 14–30.

Symphonie pathétique, 1935. Eng. tr., *Pathetic Symphony; a Tschaikovsky Novel*, London, Gollancz, 1938.

MANN, THOMAS

Buddenbrooks, 1901. Eng. tr., same title, New York, Knopf, 1924.

Denken und Leben, 1941. Eng. tr., "Thought and Life," in *American Scholar*, X (1940–41), 410–415.

Dieser Friede, 1938. Eng. tr., *This Peace*, New York, Knopf, 1938.

"Die Ehe im Übergang" (from Keyserling, H. von, *Das Ehe-Buch*, 1925). Eng. tr., "Marriage in Transition," in Keyserling, H. von, *Book of Marriage*, New York, Harcourt, Brace, 1926.

"The End," in *Free World*, IX (no. 3, 1945), 15–18.

"Germany's Guilt and Mission," in *Decision*, II (no. 1, 1941), 9–14.

Das Gesetz, 1942. Eng. tr., "Thou Shalt Have No Other Gods Before Me," in Robinson, A. L., ed., *The Ten Commandments*, New York, Simon & Schuster, 1943.

[Same.] *The Tables of the Law*, tr. H. T. Lowe-Porter, New York, Knopf, 1945.

Goethe als Repräsentant des bürgerlichen Zeitalters, 1932. Eng. tr., "Goethe," in *Yale Review*, XXI (1932), 711–735.

Herr und Hund, 1919. Eng. tr., *A Man and His Dog*, New York, Knopf, 1930. (British ed., *Bashan and I.*)

"How to Win the Peace," in *Atlantic Monthly*, CLXIX (1942), 176–183.

"In Memory of Max Liebermann, in *Catalogue, Memorial Exhibition, Max Liebermann*, Galerie St. Etienne, New York, 1944.

"The Joseph Novels," in *Atlantic Monthly*, CLXXI (Feb., 1943), 92–100.

Joseph und seine Brüder, 1933–44. Vol. I: *Die Geschichten Jaakobs*. Eng. tr., *Joseph and His Brothers*, New York, Knopf, 1936. Vol. II: *Der junge Joseph*. Eng. tr., *Young Joseph*, New York, Knopf, 1935. Vol. III: *Joseph in Ägypten*. Eng. tr., *Joseph in Egypt*, New York, Knopf, 1938. Vol. IV: *Joseph der Ernährer*. Eng. tr., *Joseph the Provider*, New York, Knopf, 1944.

Königliche Hoheit, 1909. Eng. tr., *Royal Highness*, New York, Knopf, 1939.

Lebensabriss, 1930. Eng. tr., *A Sketch of My Life*. Paris, Harrison, 1930.

"Literature and Hitler," in *Modern Thinker*, V (1934), 105–109.

The Living Thoughts of Schopenhauer Presented by Thomas Mann, New York, Longmans, Green, 1939.

Lotte in Weimar, 1939. Eng. tr., *The Beloved Returns*, New York, Knopf, 1940. (British ed., *Lotte in Weimar.*)

Mario und der Zauberer, 1930. Eng. tr., *Mario and the Magician*, New York, Knopf, 1931.

Pariser Rechenschaft, 1926. Excerpts tr. in *Dial*, LXXXII (1927), 501–510.

"The Problem of Freedom," in *Association of American Colleges Bulletin*, XXV (1939), 475–483.

"Speech Delivered at 3d American Writers Congress, 1939," in *Twice-a-Year*, no. 3–4 (1939), 135–137.

The Theme of the Joseph Novels, Washington, D.C., U.S. Govt. Print. Off., 1943.

This War, New York, Knopf, 1940.

Der Tod in Venedig, 1913. Eng. tr., *Death in Venice*, New York, Knopf, 1930.

Unordnung und frühes Leid, 1926. Eng. tr., *Early Sorrow*, New York, Knopf, 1930.

Die vertauschten Köpfe, 1940. Eng. tr., *The Transposed Heads*, New York, Knopf, 1941.

Vom zukünftigen Sieg der Demokratie, 1938. Eng. tr., *The Coming Victory of Democracy*, New York, Knopf, 1938.

"War and the Future," *Decision*, I (no. 2, 1941), 11–18.

Was ist Deutsch? Eng. tr., "What Is German?" in *Atlantic Monthly*, CLXXIII (May, 1944), 78–85.

Der Zauberberg, 1924. Eng. tr., *The Magic Mountain*, New York, Knopf, 1927.

COLLECTIONS

Freud, Goethe, Wagner, New York, Knopf, 1937.

Contents—Freud and the Future; The Sufferings and Greatness of Richard Wagner; Goethe's Career as a Man of Letters.

Listen, Germany! New York, Knopf, 1943.

Order of the Day; Political Essays, New York, Knopf, 1942.

Contents—Address Before the Emergency Rescue Committee; An Appeal to Reason; A Brother; The Coming Victory of Democracy; Culture and Politics; Europe Beware; An Exchange of Letters; The German Republic; I Stand with the Spanish People; "Mass und Wert"; Niemöller; Thinking and Living; This Peace; This War; The War and the Future; What I Believe.

Past Masters and Other Papers, New York, Knopf, 1933.

Contents—Cosmopolitanism; Culture and Socialism; Dürer; Freud's Position in the History of Modern Thought; Goethe, Novelist; Joseph Conrad's "The Secret Agent"; Lessing; Nietzsche and Music; On the Film; On the Theory of Spengler; Sleep, Sweet Sleep; The Sufferings and Greatness of Richard Wagner; Tolstoi.

Stories of Three Decades, New York, Knopf, 1938.

Contents—At the Prophet's; The Blood of the Walsungs; Death in Venice; The Dilettante; Disillusionment; Disorder and Early Sorrow; Felix Krull; The Fight Between Jappe and Do Escobar; Fiorenza; Gladius Dei; A Gleam; The Hungry; The Infant Prodigy; Little Herr Friedemann; Little Lizzy; A Man and His Dog; Mario and the Magician; A Railway Accident; Tobias Mindernickel; Tonio Kröger; Tristan; The Wardrobe; The Way to the Churchyard; A Weary Hour.

Three Essays, New York, Knopf, 1929.

Contents—An Experience in the Occult; Frederick the Great and the Grand Coalition; Goethe and Tolstoy.

REFERENCES

Beach, J. W., *The Twentieth Century Novel,* New York, Century, 1932, pp. 106–117.

Brennan, J. G., *Thomas Mann's World,* New York, Columbia Univ. Press, 1942.

Buck, P. M., *Directions in Contemporary Literature,* New York, Oxford Univ. Press, 1942, pp. 291–314.

Burkhard, A., "Thomas Mann's Appraisal of the Poet," *PMLA,* XLVI (1931), 880–916.

Cleugh, J., *Thomas Mann,* London, Secker, 1933.

Gronicka, A. von, "Thomas Mann and Russia," *Germanic Review,* XX (1945), 105–137.

Hofe, H. von, "Literature in Exile: Thomas Mann," *German Quarterly,* XVII (1944), 145–154.

Hoffmann, F. J., *Freudianism and the Literary Mind,* Baton Rouge, Louisiana State Univ. Press, 1945, pp. 181–229.

Kaufmann, F., "The World as Will and Representation: Thomas Mann's Philosophical Novels," *Philosophy and Phenomenological Research,* IV (1943–44), 1–35, 287–315.

Kohn-Bramstedt, E., "The Intellectual as Ironist," *Contemporary Review,* CLV (1939), 470–479.

Lewisohn, L., "Thomas Mann," *English Journal,* XXII (1933), 527–535.

Loose, G., "Thomas Mann and the Problem of Decadence," *University of Colorado Studies,* Ser. B, I (1941), 345–376.

Mann, E., and K. Mann, "Portrait of Our Father," *Atlantic Monthly,* CLXIII (1939), 441–451.

March, G., "Thomas Mann and the Novel of Decadence," *Sewanee Review,* XXVII (1929), 490–503.

Slochower, *No Voice Is Wholly Lost,* pp. 332–367.

Slochower, H., *Thomas Mann's Joseph Story,* New York, Knopf, 1938.

Venable, U., "Poetic Reason in Thomas Mann," *Virginia Quarterly,* XIV (1938), 61–76.

Weigand, H. J., *Thomas Mann's Novel, Der Zauberberg,* New York, Appleton–Century, 1933.

Wilkinson, E. M., in Mann, Thomas, *Tonio Kröger,* Oxford, Blackwell, 1944, pp. vii–xliv.

MEHRING, WALTER

No Road Back, Poems, New York, S. Curl, 1944.

MELL, MAX

Das Apostelspiel, 1923. Eng. tr., *Apostle Play,* London, Methuen, 1934.

REFERENCE

Lissau, R., "Recent Austrian Literature," *German Life and Letters,* IV (1939), 35–45.

MEYER, CONRAD FERDINAND

(For translations see Morgan's *Critical Bibliography,* pp. 330–331, 739.)

REFERENCES

Burkhard, A., *Conrad Ferdinand Meyer, the Style and the Man,* Cambridge, [Mass.], Harvard Univ. Press, 1932.

Klenze, *From Goethe to Hauptmann,* pp. 130–155.

Pfeiffer, F. L., "Gottfried Keller and Conrad Ferdinand Meyer," *Germanic Review,* II (1927), 312–319.

MIEGEL, AGNES

SELECTIONS

Bithell, *Contemporary German Poetry.*
Francke, *German Classics,* Vol. XVIII.
Münsterberg, *Harvest of German Verse.*

REFERENCE

Aron, A. W., "Some Tendencies in the Modern German Ballad," *Philological Quarterly,* VI (1927), 270–277.

MORGENSTERN, CHRISTIAN

SELECTIONS

Bithell, *Contemporary German Poetry.*

Deutsch and Yarmolinsky, *Contemporary German Poetry.*

REFERENCES

Delp, W. E., "Christian Morgenstern," *Modern Languages,* XXIV (1942), 17–25.

Morgan, B. Q., "The Superior Nonsense of Christian Morgenstern," *Books Abroad,* XII (1938), 288–291.

MUSIL, ROBERT

Nachlass zu Lebzeiten, 1936. Excerpt tr. as "The Fly Paper," in *German Life and Letters,* II (1937–38), 226–227.

REFERENCE

Lehner, F., "Robert Musil," *Books Abroad,* XVII (1943), 131–132.

NADLER, JOSEF

REFERENCE

Wirth, O., *Wilhelm Scherer, Josef Nadler, and Wilhelm Dilthey as Literary Historians,* dissertation, Univ. of Chicago, 1938.

NEUMANN, ALFRED

Guerra, 1929. Eng. tr., same title, New York, Knopf, 1930.
Der Held, 1930. Eng. tr., *The Hero,* New York, Knopf, 1931.
Kaiserreich, 1936. Eng. tr., *Gaudy Empire,* New York, Knopf, 1937. (British ed., *Man of December.*)
König Haber, 1926. Eng. tr., *King Haber,* New York, King, 1930.

Contents—King Haber; Schoolmaster Taussig; The Patriot.

Königin Christine von Schweden, 1935. Eng. tr., *Life of Christina of Sweden*, London, Hutchinson, 1935.

Narrenspiegel, 1932. Eng. tr., *Mirror of Fools*, New York, Knopf, 1933.

Neuer Caesar, 1934. Eng. tr., *Another Caesar*, New York, Knopf, 1935. (British ed., *New Caesar*.)

Der Patriot, 1925. Eng. tr., *The Patriot*. New York, Boni & Liveright, 1928.

Rebellen, 1929. Eng. tr., *The Rebels*, New York, Knopf, 1929.

Der Teufel, 1926. Eng. tr., *The Devil*, New York, Knopf, 1928. (British ed., *The Deuce*.)

Volksfreunde, 1941. Eng. tr., *Friends of the People*, New York, Macmillan, 1942.

NIETZSCHE, FRIEDRICH

Complete Works, New York, Macmillan, 1925, 17 vols.

REFERENCES

Bentley, E. R., *A Century of Hero Worship*, New York, Lippincott, 1944, pp. 81–152.

Brinton, C., *Nietzsche*, Cambridge, [Mass.], Harvard Univ. Press, 1941.

Closs, *Genius of the German Lyric*, pp. 372 ff.

Faguet, E., *On Reading Nietzsche*, New York, Moffat, 1918.

Fairley, B., "Nietzsche," *Queen's Quarterly*, XXXVII (1930), 259–275.

——, "Nietzsche and the Poetic Impulse," *John Rylands Library Bulletin*, XIX (1935), 344–361.

Foster, G. B., "Nietzsche and Wagner," *Sewanee Review*, XXXII (1924), 15–29.

Lichtenberger, H., "Nietzsche and the Present Crisis of Civilization," *Hibbert Journal*, XXXIV (1936), 321–330.

Mencken, H. L., *The Philosophy of Friedrich Nietzsche*, 3d ed., Boston, Luce, 1913.

Morgan, G. A., *What Nietzsche Means*, Cambridge, [Mass.], Harvard Univ. Press, 1941.

Rehder, Helmut, "Nietzsche and His Place in German Literature," *Monatshefte für deutschen Unterricht*, XXXVI (1944), 425–445.

PONTEN, JOSEF

REFERENCES

Hagboldt, P., "Josef Ponten," *German Quarterly*, III (1930), 1–14.

Shears, L. A., "The Novellen of Josef Ponten," *Germanic Review*, XI (1936), 50–55.

RAABE, WILHELM

Abu Telfan oder die Heimkehr vom Mondgebirge, 1867. Eng. tr., *Abu Telfan; Return from the Mountains of the Moon*, London, Chapman & Hall, 1881.

Der Hungerpastor, 1864. Eng. tr., *The Hunger-Pastor*, London, Chapman & Hall, 1885. (Also in Francke, *German Classics*, Vol. XI.)

REFERENCES

Silz, W., "Freytag's 'Soll und Haben' and Raabe's 'Der Hungerpastor,'" *Modern Language Notes*, XXXIX (1924), 10–17.

——, "Pessimism in Raabe's Stuttgart Trilogy," *PMLA*, XXXIX (1924), 687–704.

REMARQUE, ERICH MARIA

Drei Kameraden, 1937. Eng. tr., *Three Comrades*, Boston, Little, Brown, 1937.

Flotsam, Boston, Little, Brown, 1941.

Im Westen nichts Neues, 1929. Eng. tr., *All Quiet on the Western Front*, New York, Grosset & Dunlap, 1930.

"Strange Home," in *Best Short Stories of the War*, New York, Harper, 1931.

Der Weg zurück, 1931. Eng. tr., *The Road Back*, Boston, Little, Brown, 1931.

REFERENCE

Pfeiler, *War and the German Mind*, pp. 140–144.

RENN, LUDWIG (i.e., Vieth von Golssenau, A. F.)

Krieg, 1928. Eng. tr., *War*, New York, Dodd, Mead, 1929.

Nachkrieg, 1930. Eng. tr., *After War*, New York, Dodd, Mead, 1931.

Vor grossen Wandlungen, 1936. Eng. tr., *Death Without Battle*, New York, Dodd, Mead, 1937.

Warfare; the Relation of War to Society, New York, Oxford Univ. Press, 1939.

REFERENCES

"Ludwig Renn," *International Literature* (Moscow), 1939, no. 6, 87–88.

"Ludwig Renn, Germany's Proletarian Novelist," *Living Age*, CCCXLIII (1933), 509–512.

Pfeiler, *War and the German Mind*, pp. 159–162.

RILKE, RAINER MARIA

"Alkestis" (from *Neue Gedichte*, 1907). Eng. tr., "Alcestis," in *Accent*, IV (1943), 9–11.

Die Aufzeichnungen des Malte Laurids Brigge, 1910. Eng. tr., *Journal of My Other Self*, New York, Norton, 1930. (British ed., *The Notebook of Malte Laurids Brigge.*)

Auguste Rodin, 1903, 1913. Eng. tr., same title, New York, Sunwise Turn, 1919.

[Same.] *Auguste Rodin*, tr. J. Lemont and H. Transil, New York, Fine Editions Press, 1945.

Duineser Elegien, 1923. Eng. tr., *Duineser Elegien, Elegies from the Castle of Duino*, tr. V. and E. Sackville-West, London, Hogarth Press, 1931.

[Same.] *Duino Elegies*, tr. J. B. Leishman and S. Spender, New York, Norton, 1939.

[Same.] *Duino Elegies* and *Sonnets to Orpheus*, tr. J. Lemont, New York, Fine Editions Press, 1945.

Geschichten vom lieben Gott, 1900, 1904. Eng. tr., *Stories of God*, New York, Norton, 1932.

Das Marien-Leben, 1913. Eng. tr., *Life of the Virgin Mary*, Nürnberg, Verlag "Der Bund," 1922.

"O das Neue, Freunde, ist nicht dies" (from *Späte Gedichte*, 1934). Eng. tr., "Against the Age," in *Transition*, no. 2 (1927), 138.

Die Sonette an Orpheus, 1923. Eng. tr., *Sonnets to Orpheus*, tr. J. B. Leishman, London, Hogarth Press, 1936.

[Same.] *Sonnets to Orpheus*, tr. M. D. Herter Norton, New York, Norton, 1942.

[Same.] *Sonnets to Orpheus*, New York, Wittenborn, 1944.

Das Stundenbuch, 1905. Eng. tr., *Poems from the Book of Hours*, tr. B. Deutsch, Norfolk, Conn., New Directions, 1941.

Ur-Geräusch, 1919. Eng. tr., *Primal Sound and Other Prose Pieces.* Cummington, Mass., Cummington Press, 1943.

Die Weise von Liebe und Tod des Cornets Christoph Rilke, 1906. Eng. tr., *Tale of the Love and Death of Cornet Christopher Rilke*, New York, Norton, 1932.

LETTERS

Briefe an einen jungen Dichter, 1929. Eng. tr., *Letters to a Young Poet*, New York, Norton, 1934.

"From the Correspondence of Rainer Maria Rilke and Lisa Heise," *Twice-a-Year*, no. 8–9 (1942), 84–103.

Letters of Rainer Maria Rilke (1892–1910), tr. J. B. Greene and M. D. Herter Norton, New York, Norton, 1945.

Wartime Letters, New York, Norton, 1940.

SELECTIONS

Fifty Selected Poems, tr. C. F. MacIntyre, Berkeley, Calif., University of Calif. Press, 1940.

Later Poems, tr. J. B. Leishman, London, Hogarth Press, 1938.

Poems, tr. J. Lemont, New York, Wright, 1918.

Poems, tr. J. B. Leishman, London, Hogarth Press, 1934.

Poems, tr. J. Lemont, New York, Columbia Univ. Press, 1943.

Requiem, and Other Poems, tr. J. B. Leishman, London, Hogarth Press, 1935.

Selected Poems, tr. J. B. Leishman, London, Hogarth Press, 1941.

Translations from the Poetry of R. M. Rilke, tr. M. D. Herter Norton, New York, Norton, 1938.

BIBLIOGRAPHY

REFERENCES

Bowra, C. M., *The Heritage of Symbolism,* London, Macmillan, 1943, pp. 56–97.

Butler, E. M., *Rainer Maria Rilke,* Cambridge, [Eng.], University Press, 1941.

Closs, *Genius of the German Lyric,* pp. 416–423.

Fairley, B., "Rainer Maria Rilke, an Estimate," *University of Toronto Quarterly,* XI (1942), 1–14.

Goll, C., "Rainer Maria Rilke," *Twice-a-Year,* no. 5–6 (1940–41), 375–385.

Houston, G. C., "Rilke and Rodin," in *German Studies Presented to Prof. H. G. Fiedler,* Oxford, Clarendon Press, 1938, pp. 244–265.

Mason, E. C., *Rilke's Apotheosis,* Oxford, Blackwell, 1938.

Olivero, E., *R. M. Rilke, a Study in Poetry and Mysticism,* Cambridge, [Eng.], Heffer, 1931.

Pickman, H., "Rainer Maria Rilke," *Hound and Horn,* IV (1930–31), 325–365, 512–555.

Rose, W., ed., *Rainer Maria Rilke; Aspects of His Mind and Poetry,* London, Sidgwick & Jackson, 1938.

Spender, S., "Rainer Maria Rilke; an Appreciation," *London Mercury,* XXXVIII (1938), 328–332.

ROTH, JOSEPH

Der Antichrist, 1934. Eng. tr., *The Antichrist,* New York, Viking Press, 1935.

Die Flucht ohne Ende, 1927. Eng. tr., *Flight Without End,* New York, Doubleday, Doran, 1930.

Hiob, 1930. Eng. tr., *Job,* New York, Viking Press, 1931.

Die hundert Tage, 1936. Eng. tr., *Ballad of the Hundred Days,* New York, Viking Press, 1936.

Die Legende vom heiligen Trinker, 1939. Eng. tr., "The Legend of the Holy Drinker," in Mann and Kesten, *Heart of Europe.*

Radetzkymarsch, 1932. Eng. tr., *Radetzky March,* New York, Viking Press, 1933.

Tarabas, ein Gast auf dieser Erde, 1934. Eng. tr., *Tarabas, a Guest on Earth,* New York, Viking Press, 1934.

REFERENCES

Werner, A., "Four Tragic Jews," *Jewish Outlook*, VI (no. 5, 1941–42), 7–9.

Zweig, F., "Joseph Roth and the Zweigs," *Books Abroad*, XVIII (1944), 5–8.

SAAR, FERDINAND von

Die Steinklopfer, 1873. Eng. tr., "The Stonebreakers," in Patten, W., *Short Story Classics (Foreign)*, New York, Collier, 1907, Vol. III.

Die Troglodytin, 1888. Eng. tr., "The Troglodyte," in Busch, *Selected Austrian Short Stories*.

REFERENCE

Shears, L. A., "Theme and Technique in the Novellen of Ferdinand von Saar," *Journal of English and Germanic Philology*, XXIV (1925), 398–408.

SCHÄFER, WILHELM

"Die Frau von Stein" (from 33 *Anekdoten*, 1911). Eng. tr., "Frau von Stein," in Steinhauer and Jessiman, *Modern German Short Stories*.

SCHAEFFER, ALBRECHT

Der höllische Sebastian, 1928. Eng. tr., "Sebastian, the Black Devil," in Eaton, R., ed., *Best European Short Stories of 1928*, New York, Dodd, Mead, 1929.

SCHAUKAL, RICHARD von

SELECTIONS

Bithell, *Contemporary German Poetry*.

REFERENCE

Thomas, R. H., "Richard von Schaukal: a Poet of Austria in Decline," *German Life and Letters*, III (1938–39), 145–151.

SCHAUMANN, RUTH

SELECTIONS

Literary Digest, XCVIII (July 28, 1928), 26.

SCHICKELE, RENÉ

Das Erbe am Rhein, 1925–27. Vol. I: *Maria Capponi.* Eng. tr., same title, New York, Knopf, 1928. Vol. II: *Blick auf die Vogesen.* Eng. tr., *Heart of Alsace,* New York, Knopf, 1929.

Himmlische Landschaft, 1933. Excerpt tr. as "A Date to Remember," in *Twice-a-Year,* no. 3–4, (1939–40), 32.

Symphonie für Jazz, 1929. Excerpt tr. as "Angelica," in Mann and Kesten, *Heart of Europe.*

SELECTIONS

Transition, no. 2 (1927), 141.

REFERENCE

Schickele, R., "René Schickele," *Books Abroad,* XV (1941), 273–275.

SCHMIDTBONN, WILHELM

"Die Letzte" (from *Die Uferleute,* 1903). Eng. tr., "Derelict," in Steinhauer and Jessiman, *Modern German Short Stories.*

SCHNITZLER, ARTHUR

Amerika, 1889. Eng. tr., "America," in *Decision,* III (no. 1–2, 1942), 35–36.

Das Schicksal des Freiherrn von Leisenbogh, 1903. Eng. tr., "The Fate of the Baron," in Maugham, W. S., ed., *Tellers of Tales,* New York, Doubleday, Doran, 1939.

Über Krieg und Frieden, 1939. Eng. tr., "Notes on War and Peace," in *Twice-a-Year,* no. 3–4 (1939–40), 18–31.

Das weite Land, 1911. Eng. tr., "The Vast Domain," in *Poet Lore,* XXXIV (1923), 317–407.

(For other translations see Morgan's *Critical Bibliography,* pp. 439–441, 752.)

REFERENCES

Gross, F., "Arthur Schnitzler," *Contemporary Review,* CLI (1937), 607–612.

Liptzin, S., *Arthur Schnitzler,* New York, Prentice-Hall, 1932.

Nesbit, L., "Arthur Schnitzler," *Medical Life,* XLII (1935), 511–550.

Schinnerer, O. P., "The Early Works of Arthur Schnitzler," *Germanic Review,* IV (1929), 153–197.

Slochower, *No Voice Is Wholly Lost,* pp. 24–32.

SCHÜCKING, LEVIN LUDWIG

"The Baroque Character of the Elizabethan Tragic Hero," *Proceedings of the British Academy,* 1938, XXIV (1939), 85–111.

Die Charakterprobleme bei Shakespeare, 1919. Eng. tr., *Character Problems in Shakespeare's Plays,* London, Harrap, 1922.

Der Sinn des Hamlet, 1935. Eng. tr., *The Meaning of Hamlet,* London, Oxford Univ. Press, 1937.

Die Soziologie der literarischen Geschmacksbildung, 1923. Eng. tr., *Sociology of Literary Taste,* New York, Oxford Univ. Press, 1944.

SCHUMANN, GERHARD

SELECTIONS

German Life and Letters, III (1938–39), 298–299.

REFERENCE

Hayens, K. C., "Gerhard Schumann, Poet of the Third Reich," *German Life and Letters,* III (1938–39), 62–70.

SEGHERS, ANNA (i.e., Netty Radvanyi)

Aufstand der Fischer von St. Barbara, 1928. Eng. tr., *Revolt of the Fishermen,* New York, Longmans, Green, 1930.

Das siebte Kreuz, 1942. Eng. tr., *The Seventh Cross,* Boston, Little, Brown, 1944.

Transit, Boston, Little, Brown, 1944.

REFERENCE

Slochower, *No Voice Is Wholly Lost,* pp. 287–291.

SORGE, REINHARD JOHANNES

REFERENCE

Thomas, R. H., "Notes on Some Unpublished Papers of R. J. Sorge; a Contribution Relating to the Genesis of Expressionism," *Modern Language Review,* XXXII (1937), 423–429.

SPENGLER, OSWALD

Jahre der Entscheidung, 1933. Eng. tr., *The Hour of Decision,* New York, Knopf, 1934.

Der Mensch und die Technik, 1931. Eng. tr., *Man and Technics,* New York, Knopf, 1932.

Der Untergang des Abendlandes, 1918–22. Eng. tr., *Decline of the West,* New York, Knopf, 1926, 1928, 2 vols. (Abridged ed., *Today and Destiny,* New York, Knopf, 1940.)

REFERENCES

Adorno, T. W., "Spengler To-day," *Studies in Philosophy and Social Science,* IX (1941), 305–325.

Bentley, E. R., *A Century of Hero Worship,* New York, Lippincott, 1944, pp. 205–213.

Clark, F., "Oswald Spengler," *London Mercury,* XX (1929), 277–288.

Dreher, C., "Spengler and the Third Reich," *Virginia Quarterly Review,* XV (1939), 176–193.

Goddard, E. H., and P. A. Gibbons, *Civilization or Civilizations; a Concise Interpretation of Spengler's Philosophy of History,* New York, Boni & Liveright, 1927.

SPITTELER, CARL

(For translations see Morgan's *Critical Bibliography,* pp. 460, 756.)

REFERENCES

Boyd, E. A., *Studies from Ten Literatures,* New York, Scribner's, 1925.

Butler, *Tyranny of Greece over Germany,* pp. 316–322.

Muirhead, J. F., "Carl Spitteler," *London Mercury,* XVI (1927), 53–61.

——, "Carl Spitteler and the New Epic," *Royal Society of Literature, Essays,* X (1931), 35–57.

Robertson, J. G., *Essays and Addresses,* London, Routledge, 1935.

STADLER, ERNST

SELECTIONS

Deutsch and Yarmolinsky, *Contemporary German Poetry.*

REFERENCE

Schumann, D. W., "Ernst Stadler and German Expressionism," *Journal of English and Germanic Philology,* XXIX (1930), 510–534.

STEHR, HERMANN

REFERENCES

Hentschel, C., "Hermann Stehr," *German Life and Letters,* III (1939), 94–106.

Kaufmann, F. W., "The Style of Hermann Stehr in Its Relation to His View of Life," *Germanic Review,* VII (1932), 359–366.

Reichart, W. A., "Hermann Stehr and His Work," *Philological Quarterly,* X (1931), 47–61.

STERNHEIM, CARL

Busekow, 1928. Eng. tr., same title, in *Transition,* no. 1 (1927), 36–56.

Fairfax, 1921. Eng. tr., same title, New York, Knopf, 1923.

Die Hose, 1911. Eng. tr., "A Pair of Drawers," in *Transition,* no. 6 (1927), 16–39; no. 7 (1927), 88–102; no. 8 (1927), 97–113; no. 9 (1927), 102–119.

Die Marquise von Arcis, 1920. Eng. tr., *The Mask of Virtue,* New York, French, 1935.

Schuhlin, 1927. Eng. tr., "Schuhlin, the Musician," in Eaton, R., ed., *Best Continental Short Stories of 1927,* New York, Dodd, Mead, 1928.

Der Snob, 1913. Eng. tr., "A Place in the World," in Katzin, W., comp., *Eight European Plays,* New York, Brentano's, 1927.

REFERENCE

Drake, W. A., *Contemporary European Writers,* New York, Day, 1928, pp. 152–156.

STORM, THEODOR

(For translations see Morgan's *Critical Bibliography,* pp. 473–474, 760.)

REFERENCES

Coenen, F., "Problems in Theodor Storm's Novellen," *Germanic Review,* XV (1940), 32–45.

Wooley, E. O., "Studies in Theodor Storm," *Indiana University Publications,* Humanistic ser., no. 10 (1942).

STRAMM, AUGUST

Die Haidebraut, 1914. Eng. tr., "Bride of the Moor," in *Poet Lore,* XXV (1914), 499–513.

Sancta Susanna, 1914. Eng. tr., "Sancta Susanna, the Song of a May Night," in *Poet Lore,* XXV (1914), 514–522.

STRAUSS, EMIL

Mara, 1909. Eng. tr., same title, in Francke, *German Classics,* Vol. XIX.

SUDERMANN, HERMANN

Purzelchen, 1928. Eng. tr., *The Dance of Youth,* New York, Liveright, 1930.

(For other translations see Morgan's *Critical Bibliography,* 476–478, 760.)

REFERENCES

Coar, J. F., *Studies in German Literature in the XIX Century,* New York, Macmillan, 1903, pp. 315–335.

Diamond, W., "Hermann Sudermann," *Monatshefte für deutschen Unterricht,* XXI (1929), 155–163.

Dukes, A., *Modern Dramatists,* London, Palmer, 1911, pp. 68–78.

Huneker, J. G., *Iconoclasts,* New York, Scribner's, 1922.

Phelps, W. L., *Essays on Modern Novelists,* New York, Macmillan, 1927.

THOMA, LUDWIG

Der heilige Hies, 1904. Eng. tr., "Matt, the Holy," in Francke, *German Classics,* Vol. XIX.

Moral, 1909. Eng. tr., "Moral," in Dickinson, T. H., ed., *Chief Contemporary Dramatists,* 2d ser., Boston, Houghton Mifflin, 1921.

Lottchens Geburtstag, 1911. Eng. tr., "When You Are Twenty-One," in *One-Act Plays Monthly,* I (1937), 304–322.

"Onkel Franz" (from *Lausbubengeschichten,* 1904). Eng. tr., "Uncle Franz," in Maugham, W. S., ed., *Tellers of Tales,* New York, Doubleday, Doran, 1939.

REFERENCE

Diamond, W., "Ludwig Thoma," *Monatshefte für deutschen Unterricht,* XXI (1929), 97–101.

TOLLER, ERNST

Die blinde Göttin, 1932. Eng. tr., *The Blind Goddess,* London, Lane, 1934. (An adaptation, *Blind Man's Buff,* was issued in London by Lane, 1938, and in New York by Random House, 1939.)

Briefe aus dem Gefängnis, 1935. Eng. tr., *Look Through the Bars; Letters from Prison, Poems, and a New Version of "The Swallow Book,"* New York, Farrar & Rinehart, 1937. (British ed., *Letters from Prison.*)

Feuer aus den Kesseln, 1930. Eng. tr., *Draw the Fires,* London, Lane, 1935.

Hinkemann, 1923. Eng. tr., *Brokenbrow,* London, Nonesuch Press, 1926.

Hoppla, wir leben! 1927. Eng. tr., *Hoppla!* London, Benn, 1928.

Eine Jugend in Deutschland, 1933. Eng. tr., *I Was a German,* New York, Morrow, 1934.

Die Maschinenstürmer, 1922. Eng. tr., *The Machine-Wreckers,* New York, Knopf, 1923. (Also in Moses, M. J., ed., *Dramas of Modernism,* Boston, Little, Brown, 1941.)

Masse Mensch, 1921. Eng. tr., *Masses and Man,* London, Lane, 1934. (Also in Watson, E. B., ed., *Contemporary Drama,* New York, Scribner's, 1941.)

Nie wieder Friede! Eng. tr., *No More Peace,* New York, Farrar & Rinehart, 1937.

Quer durch, 1930. Eng. tr. of Sections 1–2, *Which World—Which Way? Travel Pictures from America and Russia,* London, Low, Marston & Co., 1931.

Die Rache des verhöhnten Liebhabers, 1925. Eng. tr., "The Scorned Lover's Revenge," in Bourne, J., ed., *Eight New One-Act Plays of 1935,* London, Dickson, 1935.

Das Schwalbenbuch, 1923. Eng. tr., *The Swallow-Book,* London, Oxford Univ. Press, 1924. (A few excerpts in *Twice-a-Year,* no. 3–4 [1939–40], 117–128.)

COLLECTIONS

Seven Plays, London, Lane, 1935.

Contents—The Machine-Wreckers; Transfiguration; Masses and Man; Hinkemann; Hoppla! Such is Life!; The Blind Goddess; Draw the Fires!; Mary Baker Eddy (with H. Kesten).

Pastor Hall; Blindman's Buff, New York, Random House, 1939.

REFERENCES

Causton, B., "Plays of a Prisoner," *Fortnightly,* CXXIX (1928), 634–645.

Loving, P., "A Note on Ernst Toller," *Dial,* LXXXVI (1929), 205–210.

Pinthus, K., "Life and Death of Ernst Toller," *Books Abroad,* XIV (1940), 3–8.

Slochower, H., "Ernst Toller," *Twice-a-Year,* no. 3–4 (1939–40), 130–134.

Willibrand, W. A., *Ernst Toller, Product of Two Revolutions,* Norman, Okla., Cooperative Books, 1941.

TRAKL, GEORG

SELECTIONS

Deutsch and Yarmolinsky, *Contemporary German Poetry.*

Transition, no. 1 (1927), 131; no. 3 (1927), 146.

TRAVEN, B[RUNO]

Die Brücke im Dschungel, 1929. Eng. tr., *Bridge in the Jungle,* New York, Knopf, 1938.

Der Karren, 1932. Eng. tr., *The Carreta,* London, Chatto & Windus, 1935.

Der Schatz der Sierra Madre, 1927. Eng. tr., *The Treasure of the Sierra Madre,* New York, Knopf, 1935.

Das Totenschiff, 1926. Eng. tr., *The Death Ship,* New York, Knopf, 1934.

TROELTSCH, ERNST

Der Historismus und seine Überwindung, 1924. Eng. tr., *Christian Thought,* London, University of London Press, 1923.

(Other works have been translated.)

TÜGEL, LUDWIG

Der Wiedergänger, 1929. Eng. tr., *The Visitant,* London, Secker, 1931.

UNRUH, FRITZ von

Bonaparte, 1926. Eng. tr., *Bonaparte, a Drama,* New York, Knopf, 1928.

"Champien," in *Best Short Stories of the War,* New York, Harper, 1931.

Opfergang, 1916. Eng. tr., *Way of Sacrifice,* New York, Knopf, 1928.

REFERENCES

Pfeiler, *War and the German Mind,* pp. 90–97.

Rose, W., "Contemporary German Literature, the Younger Generation," *London Mercury,* XVI (1927), 512–524.

Simon, H., "Fritz von Unruh; Germany's New Poet," *Bermondsey Book,* II (1925), 50–59.

Stirk, *The Prussian Spirit,* pp. 82–91.

VIEBIG, CLARA (i.e., Mrs. Clara Cohn)

"Der Klingeljunge" (from *Die Rosenkranzjungfer,* 1901). Eng. tr., "The Milk Boy," in Steinhauer and Jessiman, *Modern German Short Stories.*

(For other translations see Morgan's *Critical Bibliography,* pp. 493, 763.)

WAGGERL, KARL HEINRICH

Brot, 1930. Eng. tr., *Bread,* London, Hopkinson, 1931.

REFERENCES

Lawson, M. F., "Enter Author: Erlebte Rede in the Work of Karl Heinrich Waggerl," *Monatshefte für deutschen Unterricht*, XXXII (1940), 279–288.

Lissau, R., "Recent Austrian Literature," *German Life and Letters*, IV (1939), 35–45.

WAGNER, RICHARD

(For translations see Morgan's *Critical Bibliography*, pp. 498–508, 764.)

REFERENCES

Barzun, J., *Darwin, Marx, Wagner*, Boston, Little, Brown, 1941, pp. 255–347.

Bentley, E. R., *A Century of Hero Worship*, New York, Lippincott, 1944, pp. 165–182.

Kaufmann, *German Dramatists of the 19th Century*, pp. 152–177.

Newman, E., *Life of Wagner*, New York, Knopf, 1933–.

WALZEL, OSKAR

Deutsche Romantik, 1908. Eng. tr., *German Romanticism*, New York, Putnam, 1932.

WASSERMANN, JAKOB

Das Amulett, 1927. Eng. tr., "The Amulet," in Maugham, W. S., ed., *Tellers of Tales*, New York, Doubleday, Doran, 1939.

(For other translations see Morgan's *Critical Bibiliography*, pp. 509–510, 764–765.)

REFERENCES

Blankenagel, J. C., *The Writings of Jakob Wassermann*, Boston, Christopher Pub. House, 1942.

Gross, F., "Jakob Wassermann," *Contemporary Review*, CLIV (1938), 327–333.

WEBER, MAX

Gesammelte Aufsätze zur Religionssoziologie, 1920. Eng. tr. of Vol. I, *Protestant Ethic and the Spirit of Capitalism*, London, Allen & Unwin, 1930.

WEDEKIND, FRANK

Der greise Freier, 1905. Eng. tr., *The Grisly Suitor,* Philadelphia, Brown Bros., 1911.

Totentanz, 1906. Eng. tr., "The Virgin and the White Slaver," in *International,* VII (1913), 279–282.

(For other translations see Morgan's *Critical Bibliography,* pp. 511–512, 765.)

REFERENCES

Dukes, A., *Modern Dramatists,* London, Palmer, 1911, pp. 95–113.

Heuser, F. W. J., "Gerhart Hauptmann and Frank Wedekind," *Germanic Review,* XX (1945), 55–68.

Samuel, H. B., *Modernities,* New York, Dutton, 1914.

Theis, O. F., "Frank Wedekind," *Poet Lore,* XXIV (1913), 237–247.

WEHNER, JOSEF MAGNUS

"Red Light of Morning," in *Best Short Stories of the War,* New York, Harper, 1931.

WEINHEBER, JOSEF

Späte Krone, 1936. Excerpts tr. in *German Life and Letters,* II (1937–38), 306–308.

REFERENCE

Hofrichter, R., *Three Poets and Reality,* New Haven, Yale Univ. Press, 1942, pp. 43–69.

WERFEL, FRANZ

Der Abituriententag, 1928. Eng. tr., *Class Reunion,* New York, Simon & Schuster, 1929.

Barbara oder die Frömmigkeit, 1929. Eng. tr., *The Pure in Heart,* New York, Simon & Schuster, 1931. (British ed., *Hidden Child.*)

Die Blassblaue Frauenhandschrift, 1940. Eng. tr., *April in October,* in *American Magazine,* CXXXVII (1940), 48–80.

Bocksgesang, 1921. Eng. tr., *Goat Song,* Garden City, N.Y., Doubleday, Page, 1926. (Also in *Theatre Guild Anthology,* New York, Random House, 1936.)

BIBLIOGRAPHY

"From a Discourse on a Religious Experience," in *Transition,* no. 23 (1935), 87–88.

Die Geschwister von Neapel, 1931. Eng. tr., *The Pascarella Family,* New York, Simon & Schuster, 1932.

Höret die Stimme, 1937. Eng. tr., *Hearken unto the Voice,* New York, Viking Press, 1938.

Jacobowsky und der Oberst, 1944. Eng. tr., *Jacobowsky and the Colonel,* New York, Viking Press, 1944.

Juarez und Maximilian, 1924. Eng. tr., *Juarez and Maximilian,* New York, Simon & Schuster, 1926.

Das Lied von Bernadette, 1941. Eng. tr., *The Song of Bernadette,* New York, Viking Press, 1942.

Paulus unter den Juden, 1926. Eng. tr., *Paul Among the Jews,* London, Diocesan House, 1928.

Realismus und Innerlichkeit, 1931; *Können wir ohne Gottesglauben leben?* 1932; *Von der reinsten Glückseligkeit des Menschen,* 1938; *Theologumena,* 1944. Eng. tr., *Between Heaven and Earth,* New York, Philosophical Library, 1944.

Die schlimme Legende vom gerissenen Galgenstrick. Eng. tr., "The Bulletproof Hidalgo," in Mann and Kesten, *Heart of Europe.*

"Thanks," in *Decision,* I (1941), 42–43.

"Thou shalt not take the name of the Lord thy God in vain," in Robinson, A. L., ed., *The Ten Commandments,* New York, Simon & Schuster, 1943.

Der Tod des Kleinbürgers, 1927. Eng. tr., *The Man Who Conquered Death,* New York, Simon & Schuster, 1927.

Verdi: Briefe, 1926. (Ed. with P. Stefan.) Eng. tr., *Verdi, the Man in His Letters,* New York, L. B. Fischer, 1942.

Verdi: Roman der Oper, 1924. Eng. tr., *Verdi: a Novel of the Opera,* New York, Simon & Schuster, 1925.

Der veruntreute Himmel, 1939. Eng. tr., *Embezzled Heaven,* Garden City, N.Y., Sun Dial Press, 1942.

Die vierzig Tage des Musa Dagh, 1933. Eng. tr., *The Forty Days of Musa Dagh,* New York, Modern Library, 1937.

Der Weg der Verheissung, ein Bibelspiel, 1935. Eng. tr., *The Eternal Road,* New York, Viking Press, 1936.

COLLECTION

Twilight of a World, New York, Viking Press, 1937.
Contents—Poor People; Class Reunion; Estrangement; Saverio's Secret; The Staircase; The Man Who Conquered Death; The House of Mourning; Not the Murderer.

REFERENCES

Drake, W. A., *Contemporary European Writers,* New York, Day, 1928, pp. 28–42.

Hofe, H. von., "Literature in Exile: Franz Werfel," *German Quarterly,* XVII (1944), 263–272.

Kohn-Bramstedt, E., "Franz Werfel as a Novelist," *Contemporary Review,* CXLVI (1934), 66–73.

Mayer-Haas, K., "Franz Werfel," *The Bermondsey Book,* III (1926), 72–80.

Schumann, D., "The Development of Werfel's 'Lebensgefühl' as Reflected in His Poetry," *Germanic Review,* VI (1931), 27–53.

Stamm, I. A., "Religious Experience in Werfel's 'Barbara,' " *PMLA,* LIV (1939), 332–347.

WIECHERT, ERNST EMIL

Die Majorin, 1934. Eng. tr., *The Baroness,* New York, Norton, 1936.

REFERENCES

Baer, L., "A Study of Ernst Wiechert," *Modern Language Quarterly,* V (1944), 469–480.

Forster, R. L., "The Conservative Elements in German Literature," *Contemporary Review,* CLIX (1941), 198–205.

Meyer, S., "The Plow and the Soil in Ernst Wiechert's Works," *Monatshefte für deutschen Unterricht,* XXX (1938), 314–319.

Stirk, *The Prussian Spirit,* pp. 207–214.

Workman, J. D., "Ernst Wiechert's Escapism," *Monatshefte für deutschen Unterricht,* XXXV (1943), 23–33.

WÖLFFLIN, HEINRICH

Die klassische Kunst in der italienischen Renaissance, 1889. Eng. tr., *Art of the Italian Renaissance,* New York, Putnam, 1926.

Kunstgeschichtliche Grundbegriffe, 1915. Eng. tr., *Principles of Art History,* London, Bell, 1932.

REFERENCE

Hughes, M. Y., "Zeitgeist and Style," *Sewanee Review,* XLII (1934), 482–491.

WOLF, FRIEDRICH

Doktor Mamlocks Ausweg, 1935. Eng. tr., *Professor Mamlock,* New York, Universum, 1935.

"Fascist Drama," in *International Literature* (Moscow), 1937, no. 3, 79–85.

Floridsdorf, 1935. Eng. tr., *Floridsdorf, the Vienna Workers in Revolt,* New York, Universum, 1935.

"Kiki," in *International Literature* (Moscow), 1942, no. 1–2, 42–47.

Die Matrosen von Cattaro, 1930. Eng. tr., *The Sailors of Cattaro,* New York, French, 1935.

WUNDT, WILHELM MAX

Grundriss der Psychologie, 1896. Eng. tr., *Outlines of Psychology,* New York, Stechert, 1902.

(Other works have been translated.)

ZECH, PAUL

"Homeland in the Jungle," in *Living Age,* CCCLIII (1937), 159–162.

"A Village Without Men," in *International Literature* (Moscow), 1935, no. 10, 28–33.

SELECTIONS

Deutsch and Yarmolinsky, *Contemporary German Poetry.*

ZILLICH, HEINRICH

REFERENCE

Mueller, W. J., "Heinrich Zillich," *Monatshefte für deutschen Unterricht,* XXXII (1940), 198–204.

ZUCKMAYER, CARL

"Die Geschichte vom Lappenvogt Bal" (from *Ein Bauer aus dem Taunus und andere Geschichten,* 1927). Eng. tr., "Story of Bal, Governor of the Lapps," in Eaton, R., ed., *Best Continental Stories of 1927,* New York, Dodd, Mead, 1928.

Der Hauptmann von Köpenick, 1930. Eng. tr., *The Captain of Köpenick,* London, Bles, 1932.

Salwàre oder die Magdalena von Bozen, 1936. Eng. tr., *The Moons Ride Over,* New York, Viking Press, 1937.

Second Wind, New York, Doubleday, Doran, 1940.

REFERENCE

Stirk, *The Prussian Spirit,* pp. 97–105.

ZWEIG, ARNOLD

"Ein Bilaem" (from *Knaben und Männer,* 1931). Eng. tr., "A Balaam," in Maugham, W. S., ed., *Tellers of Tales,* New York, Doubleday, Doran, 1939.

Bilanz der deutschen Judenheit, 1933. Eng. tr., *Insulted and Exiled, the Truth About the German Jews,* London, Miles, 1937.

De Vrient kehrt heim, 1932. Eng. tr., *De Vrient Goes Home,* New York, Viking Press, 1933.

Junge Frau von 1914, 1931. Eng. tr., *Young Woman of 1914,* New York, Viking Press, 1932.

The Living Thoughts of Spinoza Presented by Arnold Zweig, New York, Longmans, Green, 1939.

Die Novellen um Claudia, 1912. Eng. tr., *Claudia,* New York, Viking Press, 1930.

"Sapper Schammes," in *International Literature* (Moscow), 1936, no. 10, 25–28.

Spielzeug der Zeit, 1933. Eng. tr., *Playthings of Time,* New York, Viking Press, 1935.

Trilogie des Übergangs, 1927–37. Vol. I: *Erziehung vor Verdun.* Eng. tr., *Education Before Verdun,* New York, Viking Press, 1936. Vol. II: *Der Streit um den Sergeanten Grischa.* Eng. tr., *The Case of Sergeant Grischa,* New York, Viking Press, 1928. Vol. III: *Einsetzung eines Königs.* Eng. tr., *The Crowning of a King,* New York, Viking Press, 1938.

REFERENCES

Fishman, S., "War Novels of Arnold Zweig," *Sewanee Review,* XLIX (1941), 433–451.

Pfeiler, *War and the German Mind,* pp. 129–139.

ZWEIG, STEFAN

Amerigo, 1942. Eng. tr., *Amerigo, a Comedy of Errors,* New York, Viking Press, 1942.

Baumeister der Welt, 1925. Eng. tr., *Master Builders, a Typology of the Spirit,* New York, Viking Press, 1939. (Separate translations have also been issued of Vols. I and III under the titles, *Three Masters: Balzac, Dickens, Dostoeffsky,* 1930, and *Adepts in Self-Portraiture: Casanova, Stendhal, Tolstoy,* 1928.)

Der begrabene Leuchter, 1936. Eng. tr., *The Buried Candelabrum,* New York, Viking Press, 1937.

Brasilien, ein Land der Zukunft, 1941. Eng. tr., *Brazil, Land of the Future,* New York, Viking Press, 1941.

Castellio gegen Calvin, 1936. Eng. tr., *The Right to Heresy: Castellio Against Calvin,* New York, Viking Press, 1936.

Emil Verhaeren, 1910. Eng. tr., same title, Boston, Houghton Mifflin, 1914.

Magellan, der Mann und seine Tat, 1938. Eng. tr., *Conqueror of the Seas; the Story of Magellan,* New York, Viking Press, 1938.

Romain Rolland, 1921. Eng. tr., same title, New York, Seltzer, 1921.

Sternstunden der Menschheit, 1927. Eng. tr., enlarged, *Tide of Fortune; Twelve Historical Miniatures,* New York, Viking Press, 1940.

Ungeduld des Herzens, 1938. Eng. tr., *Beware of Pity,* New York, Viking Press, 1939.

Verlaine, 1905. Eng. tr., *Paul Verlaine*, Boston, Luce, 1913.

The World of Yesterday, an Autobiography, New York, Viking Press, 1943.

COLLECTIONS

The Old-Book Peddler and Other Tales for Bibliophiles, Evanston, Ill., Northwestern University, 1937.

Contents—Books Are the Gateway to the World; The Old-Book Peddler; The Invisible Collection; Thanks to Books.

The Royal Game; Amok; Letter from an Unknown Woman, New York, Viking Press, 1944.

(For other translations see Morgan's *Critical Bibliography*, pp. 550, 769.)

REFERENCES

Brittin, N. A., "Stefan Zweig, Biographer and Teacher," *Sewanee Review*, XLVIII (1940), 245–254.

Liptzin, *Germany's Stepchildren*, pp. 211–225.

Romains, J., *Stefan Zweig, Great European*, New York, Viking Press, 1941.

INDEX OF NAMES

INDEX OF NAMES

INDEX OF NAMES

INDEX OF NAMES

INDEX OF GERMAN AND ENGLISH TITLES

In the Index are listed all German titles mentioned in the text, as well as the titles of all available English translations with the original titles in ( ). The English titles following the German are given in ( ) where a translation exists, and in [ ] where I have supplied the English equivalent for the convenience of the reader.

INDEX OF TITLES

INDEX OF TITLES

INDEX OF TITLES

INDEX OF TITLES

INDEX OF TITLES

INDEX OF TITLES

INDEX OF TITLES

INDEX OF TITLES

INDEX OF TITLES

INDEX OF TITLES